SOURCES OF LAW AND SOCIETY IN ANCIENT INDIA

SOURCES OF LAW AND SOCIETY IN ANCIENT INDIA

NARES CHANDRA SEN GUPTA

GYAN

Published by

Gyan Publishing House
5, Ansari Road
Daryaganj, New Delhi-110002
Phone: 011-47034999, 9811692060
E-mail: books@gyanbooks.com

Distribution Network
gyanbooks.com
India, USA, Canada, UK, Australia

ISBN: 978-93-6780-260-1 (PB)

First Published, 1914

2nd Impression 2024

Printed at: Gyan Press, Delhi.

SOURCES OF LAW AND SOCIETY IN ANCIENT INDIA
Author: NARES CHANDRA SEN GUPTA

Sources of Law and Society in Ancient India

A thesis for the degree of Doctor of Laws of the Calcutta University

BY

Nares Chandra Sen Gupta, M.A., M.L.

CALCUTTA
ART PRESS

1914

PREFACE

The following thesis is an attempt to study the sources of Ancient Indian law with reference to their environments in society. The following are the principal points, I have attempted to establish which, I believe, constitute some advance on the existing knowledge on the subject :

(*a*) Ancient Indian society was primarily an aggregate of smaller societies more or less autonomous. The village community was not the only nor the most important of such societies.

(*b*) Kingship in ancient India slowly gained in power and organised these semi-independent societies into a State.

(*c*) In the society there was an important distinction between Aryas and those who were not Aryas—the former were primarily looked upon as members of the community whom the sacred law contemplated, the rest being regarded as mere execrescenses. The sacred Aryan law did not apply to non-Aryas.

(*d*) Each society or community had a source of law common to itself and constituted its own judicial tribunal.

(*e*) Sruti as a source of law was primarily the embodiment of a theory and not a practical source of law. At a later date it rose to the position of a practical source of law.

(*f*) Smriti originally meant recollection of seer-sages and did not mean the Dharmasâstras. The conception of Smriti and the scope of its authority underwent important changes in course of time.

(*g*) Custom was distinguished as sacred and secular. Sacred custom had authority subject to Sruti and was supposed to be founded on a srauta presemption. The nature and scope of authority of various classes of sacred custom varied at different times.

(*h*) Besides sacred custom which was a source of the laws of Aryas in matters pertaining to dharma, other customs were recognised among the Aryas themselves, in matters not of spiritual import, as well as among persons outside the pale of sacred law. On these matters custom *per se* and the rules made by the communities themselves supplemented by the secular wisdom which passed under the name of Arthasâstra furnished the only body of laws. Royal decrees having force of law only prevailed outside the sphere sacred law.

In my account of the Hindu Society as depicted in the Dharmasâstras I have had occasion to insist on the integrity and autonomous constitution of a number of communities some of which I consider to be antepolitical. This may or may not countenance the views of those who hold communities to be historically antecedent to the individual, but the constitution of ancient Indian society can, I believe, only be properly understood if we take adequate account of these various societies which almost overshadow the State. I hope I have not been guilty of any exaggeration of the importance of these societies, but if there has been any absence of proportion, that was a risk I thought worth running. It is high time, as Pollock and Maitland point out (History of English Law Vol. I p. 687) that the reaction represented by communalistic view of history should be felt. For though with reference to India, the antithesis of the individual and the "sovereign one or many" has not been carried to inordinate excesses, yet the village has too often been supposed to be the only real community in India. I have attempted to show that there were other societies which, in practical life, carried equal, if not greater weight than the village.

I have also attempted to develop the legal conceptions dealt with in this thesis historically and have, I venture to hope, initiated a somewhat new method, mainly following the one indicated by Ihering with reference to Roman Law, in the study of problems of Hindu Law. Some of my conclusions such as the foundation of Aryan law on agreement, the derivation of Aryan laws from ancient colleges of men learned in religious lore and the antiquity of what I have called antepolitical societies may possibly have a bearing on general questions of Jurisprudence.

In pursuing my investigations I have received the kind assistance of Pandit Lakshmana Shastri of the Sanskrit College,

Calcutta in reading the *Tantravârttika*. In my German studies I have been assisted by my German tutor Mr. J. Falko. For the rest I have relied solely upon my own studies. The authorities from which I have mainly drawn my materials are given in the list annexed hereto. The Sanskrit books have been consulted in the original, but I owe a great deal to the many valuable translations, notably those by Bühler and Jolly. The introductions to these works have furnished much food for thought.

NARES C. SEN GUPTA.

3, DUFF LANE:
Calcutta, 30th December, 1913.

LIST OF AUTHORITIES CONSULTED.

Manu Samhita with commentaries—Ed. Mandlik.

Yajnavalkya with *Mitakshara*—Ed. Bapu Shastri Moghe.

Gautama Dharmasutra—in Manmathanath Datta's *Dharmasutras*.

Vishnu Dharmasutra—in Manmathanath Datta's *Dharmasutras*.

Baudhâyana Dharmasutra —Ed. Bühler: Leipzig, 1884.

Apastamba (with Haradatta's *Ujjala*)—Mysore Government publication.

Nârada Samhita—Ed. Jolly (Asiatic Society).

Brihaspati, Fragments of, and *Nârada*—Translation by Jolly in Sacred Books of the East.

Vasistha & Baudhâyana ; Apástamba & Gautama—Translation by Bühler *Sacred Book of the East.*

Manusamhita—Translation by Burnell and Hopkins (Trübner 1884).

Manusamhita—Translation by Bühler (S. B. E.).

History of Ancient Sanskrit Literature—Max Müller.

Darmesteter and Mills : *Zend Avesta*, Sacred Books of the East.

Dayabhaga—Ed. Chandicharan Smritibhusan.

Brihadaranyaka, Chandogya & Katha Upanishads.

Kautilya : *Arthasâstra*, Mysore Government publication.

Journal of the Royal Asiatic Society 1909—Articles by Jacobi, Oldenberg, Kennedy & Sayce on the Hittite Inscriptions.

Mimânsâ Darsana with *Sabara Bhasya*—Bibliotheca Iindica.

Tantravârttika, Benares Edition.

Vivadachintamani—Translation by Prasanna Kumar Tagore.

Hemadri, Chaurvarga Chintamani—Bibliotheca Indica.

Bryce : *Studies in History and Jurisprudence.*

Maine : *Ancient Law* with notes by Sir F. Pollock.

,, *Early Law and Custom.*

,, *Village Communities.*

,, *Early History of Institutions.*

Ihering : *Geist der Römischen Rechts.*

,, *Laws as a Means to an End* : Translation in Modern Legal Philosophy series.

Sohm : *Institutes of Roman Law.*

Justinian : *Digest* Vol. I—Translated by Munro

,, *Institutes*—Translation by Moyle.

Muirhead: *Roman Law*—Ed. Goudy.
Gaius: *Institutes*—Ed. Poste.
Miraglia: *Comparative Legal Philosophy*—Translation in Modern Legal Philosophy series.
Korkunov: *General Theory of Law.*—Translation in Modern Legal Philosophy series.
Baden Powell: *The Indian Village Community.*
Lee: *Historical Jurisprudence.*
Deussen: *Religion and Philosophy of India.*
Religious Systems of the World—(Sonnenschein).
Mommsen: *History of Rome* (Everyman's Library).
Tacitus: *Germany and Annals* (Scott Library).
Hallam: *History of the Middle Ages.*
Jenks: *Law and Politics in the Middle Ages.*
Loserth: *Geschichte der Spätcrer Mittelalters.*
Plato: *Republic* (Golden Treasury series).
Aristotle: *Politics*—Translated by J. E. C. Welldon.
Nelson: *View of Hindu Law.*
,, *Prospectus on a Scientific Study of Hindu Law.*
Innes: *An Examination of Mr. Nelson's views of Hindu Law.*
Mayne: *Hindu Law.*
West & Buhler: *Digest of Hindu Law.*
Trevelyan: *Hindu Law.*
Jogendranath Bhattacharyya: *Hindu Law* Vol. I 3rd Ed.
,, ,, *Hindu Law* 2nd Ed.
Raghunandana: *Astâbinsati Tattwa.*
Holmes: *Common Law.*
Salmond: *Jurisprudence.*
Chaldea (Story of Nations series).
Oldenberg: *Grihya sutras*, Sacred Books of the East.
Muir: *Sanskrit Texts.*
Roth: *Literature and History of the Vedas.*
Parasara Samhita (in Manmathanath Dutt's *Dharma sastras*).
Parasara with Madhava's Commentary (Bibliotheca Indica).
Apastamba, Atri, Harita, Daksha and Usanas Samhitas—in M. N. Dutta's *Dharmasastras.*
Jolly: *History of Hindu Law*—Tagore Law Lectures.
Cowell: *Hindu Law*—(Tagore Law Lecturer).
K. L. Sarkar: *The Mimansa Rules of Interpretation*—Tagore Law Lecturer).
G. C. Sarkar: *Hindu Law.*
Rigveda—Translation by Max Müller.
Burnell: *Dayabibhaga.*

Vishnu Purâna—Translation by H. H. Wilson.
H. H. Wilson: *Works.*
Vincent Smith: *Early History of India.*
Pollock and Maitland: *History and English Law.*
Viramitrodaya.
Crauford: *Researches concerning the laws etc. of Ancient and Modern India.*
Richardson: *Dhammathât.*
Encyclopediœa Brittanica: Articles on *Persia* & *Jurisprudence.*
Surendranath Sen: *Hindu Jurisprudence.*
Sudraka: *Mrichakatika.*
Compte: *Positive Philosophy*—Translation by Harriett Martineau.
Syama Charan Sarkar. *Vyavastha Darpana.*
Colebrooke: *Digest.*
Halhed: *Gentoo Law.*
F. Macnaghten: *Hindu Law.*

SOURCES OF LAW AND SOCIETY IN ANCIENT INDIA.

INTRODUCTORY.

The sources of law take up an important part of the exposition of Hindu law as of any system of ancient law which could boast of a system at all. Indeed at an early stage in the emergence of law into self consciousness in the life of a nation there comes a demand for a definition of its sources. A consideration of them is likewise of great interest both for the historical student and the practical jurist.

In an enquiry into the actual sources of law we have to be on our guard against taking any enumeration of those sources in the classical text books at more than their real worth. Early legal dicta (Rechtssätze) are merely a rough and ready way of setting out the observation and understanding by contemporary jurists of juristic facts. They are therefore apt to mislead unless we approach them from a correct point of view and are in a position to eliminate from them the sources of misunderstanding. The inperfections of the dicta arise, as Ihering points out (*a*), partly on account of deficiency in the powers of observation and expression (Beobachtungsgabe and Darstellungstalent) and partly because the authors of those dicta, writing for contemporaries, took for granted a great deal of their notorious presuppositions without a knowledge of which they might appear to posterity either as riddles or as laying down principles perhaps entirely opposed to their real purport.

Besides this common source of error in all ancient dicta, the enumerations of the sources of law labour under the further disadvantage that they are very generally not a plain presentment of the actual practical law (tatsächliche Recht) but of that as coloured by a theory. Thus for instance the Roman jurists generally agree in refering the origin of all law to the agreement of people and proceed to test the sources of law by the application of that criterion, by asking, viz., how far the source in question

---

(*a*) Ihering: Geist der Römischen Rechts VI Aufl. pp. 28 *et seq.*

may be regarded as expressing the common will of the people (*b*). So also the Hindu lawgivers all agree in refering the origin of law to a Sruti or Eternal revealed knowledge, an assumption which, so far as law proper is concerned is almost admittedly without any foundation (*c*). Starting with that assumption the Hindu jurists generally proceed to test the other sources of law by considering how far those sources may be relied upon to give the teaching of the Sruti (*d*). These secondary sources were undoubtedly sources of practical law but their respective values as they are represented from the Srauta point of view may not have exactly coincided with fact and usage. A theory is generally more or less inadequate to start with and the Sruti theory of law may well be supposed to have given a place to sources which were not practical springs of law and on the other to have excluded those to which people habitually looked for the law. It would be only with the progress of time that the inadequacy of the theory to cover all facts would become patent and then attempts would be made to revise the theory from time to time so as to reach a completer and more satisfactory conclusion.

This end, at which the enumeration of the sources of law would exactly coincide with the practical sources, would be the result of a two-fold process of approximation between theory and fact. On the one hand, the ideas of jurists on the sources of law develop an increasing amount of precision, and, on the other, the more or less general acceptance of the theory itself reacts upon the usual sources of law so that sources disapproved by theory tend to fall into disfavour and those which the theory itself has produced tend to rise into prominence. An illustration may be given from conclusions which I propose to elucidate in the course of this thesis.

So far as law proper (which was a part of the *Samayacharika* rules) was concerned, the real practical sources in pre-Dharma-

---

(*b*) See Digest Bk. I Tit III. The assumption underlying these tests viz. that law is founded on agreement Korkunov considers to be a fiction. Korkunov. *General Theory of Law* Trans. Hastings p. 411. See on this *post* Part II §3.

(*c*) See Apastamba II, 11, 29 who practically admits that so far as Samayacharika rules are concerned the Vedas furnish very little guidance. See authorities discussed post under Part II §2.

(*d*) This mode of argument is elaborated in the Mimansa Darsana, Sabara Bhasya and Kumarila's Tantra Varttika in the third Pada but it underlies all the mere enumerations of authors like Gautama, Vasistha, Bandhayana, Apastamba and others. A full discussion of the authorities will be found post under Part II §2.

sastra days were tradition and usage interpreted and enforced by various societies and among others, by the Parishads. In the earliest Dharmasastras we find that these are recognised as sources of law though the ultimate spring of their authority is referred to the Veda. This reference to the Veda is, with the earliest law-givers, little more than a formula for showing reverence to the revealed word and expressing the sanctity and supra- sensible authority of custom (*e*). They did not attempt to seek the practical law in the texts of the Vedas as they were, nor confront Vedic rules with customs or traditions. With later writers however we find an increasing tendency to refer to the dicta and the examples as embodied in the Vedas for authority till we reach perhaps the culminating point in the elevation of the Veda to the position of a direct source of practical law in the writings of authors like Sabaraswami and Kumarila Swami. Every rule of custom and Smriti is confronted wherever possible with Vedic texts and if the various authors differ as to the exact quantum of relative authority to be attached to these they take it for granted that texts of Veda are sources of absolutely binding positive law. The character of tradition and custom changes under the Sruti theory. While in works like that of Apastamba we find them enjoying almost absolute primacy amongst sources of law they dwindle in authority and are hemmed in with more and more stringent limitations till we find Kumarilaswami asserting that tradition is authority only when it comes from Rishis who are mentioned in the Vedas and usage can be considered only when it is that of persons who are found to have habitually regulated their conduct by the religious law and then only when in acting as they do in the case in question they are obviously impelled by a desire to follow the religious law and do not go against Sruti and Smriti texts (*f*).

That is how practical law tends to approximate to the theory. On the other hand, we have only got to refer to the various Dharmasastras to see how the enumeration of the springs of law tends to amplify. Thus while Gautama refers, besides Veda, to the recollections and habits of men who know the Vedas and Apastamba to the agreement of learned men, (though they

---

(*e*) See post Part II §2.

(*f*) Tantra Varttika under Pada III Sutra 7.

"वेदेनैवाभ्यानुज्ञाता येषामेव प्रवक्तृता। नित्यानामभिधेयानां मन्वन्तर युगादिषु॥

तेषां विपरिवर्त्तेषु कुर्व्वतां धर्म्मसंहिता:। वचनानि प्रमाणानि नान्येषामिति निश्चय:॥

and "धर्म्मत्वेन प्रपन्नानि शिष्टैर्यानितु कानिचित्। वैदिकै: कर्त्तृसामान्यात्तेषां धर्म्मत्वमिष्यते।

tacitly recognise other sources in the body of their works) as the only sources of law, we find the list growing fuller, more precise and more embracing as we go from these authors to Vasistha and Baudhayana and more so when we come to Manu and Yajnavalkya, This development of the theory in precision and elaborateness is the result of an attempt to approximate theory to actual facts.

Illustrations of the inadequacy of early theories to present facts in their true perspective and of the correction of the divergence between fact and theory by this two-fold process of approximation might be adduced from other systems of law. If this is a fact we cannot wholly rely upon the early enumerations of the sources of law without first being in a position to correct the errors of perspective to which these may lead us. To be able to do so and to arrive at a really complete conception of the practical law of those ancient times we shall have to take whole ancient literature in a mass and sift their legal principles and institutions to discover what Ihering calls their "inner chronology," of which time succession, even if well ascertained, would convey an imperfect idea. We shall further have to complete the legal dicta themselves by furnishing their presuppositions from a study of them with reference to their environments—the social and legal institutions of the times, the ideas of the people, the Social Ends and ideals and in short the entire culture of the time to which the dictum belonged.

The Social Ends must form an important part of our investigation specially when we have to deal not with a bare presentment of facts or actual rules but with those as coloured by a theory. Ihering has brought out the great importance of social ends in determining the contents of law (*g*). The relativity of law to ends must now be taken to be a settled fact. The relativity however extends, not only to the contents of law, as Ihering establishes, but also to its form and source, as Korkunov points out (*h*). The sources of law recognised in any system are pre-eminently determined by the ends contemplated by the society to which the law applies and vary with a change in social ends and ideals. To make a reconstruction of this character with reference to Hindu law would require the labours of experts in all branches of Sanskritic learning, of archælogists, Epigraphists,

(*g*) Ihering: Law as a means to an end. Modern Legal Philosophy series. Boston.

(*h*) Korkunov. General Theory of Law. Translation by Hastings p. 76.

Numismatists, Anthropologists and others. In this thesis all that I propose to attempt is to study the sources of Hindu law with reference to institutions and social ends of ancient India such as can be traced in the legal literature itself.

I assume of course that the law as laid down in Sanskrit works like the Smritis and developed and interpreted in commentaries and *Nibandha* works represents the law which at some time or other prevailed in ancient India, at any rate in Aryan India. I am aware that there is a class of opinion which would be chary of accepting this as a statement of fact even if it did not venture to go so far as to deny straightway that they were works of authority at any time or reflected the true state of law in any age in Indian history. Thus, for instances, Nelson, while mainly concerned with denying the authority of Sanskrit works in southern India, is obviously skeptical about the existence of any set of laws like that in the Sanskrit works anywhere at any time. This strong undercurrent of skepticism comes to the surface in his bold and unhesitating statement that that Hindus had no courts and no laws at any time (*i*). The grotesque absurdity of such a statement would be manifest when we examine the authorities which he puts forward for this proposition. The entirely negative evidence of Megasthenes and the Chinese travellers, coupled with the equally negative travellers' tales of Abbe Dubois, Marco Polo, Bernier, Tavernier, P. Van den Broeck and Father Bouchet in very modern times and with isolated and localised observations of Sir William Jones and Antequil Duperron furnish the magnificent testimony which Nelson opposes to that of an unbroken series of Sanskrit works of great antiquity. The evidence of Sir William Jones (*j*) adduced by Nelson, if studied with reference to the modes of recovery of debt mentioned by Manu and other Smriti writers (*k*), would possibly lead to the opposite conclusion and furnish a strong indication that the customs referred to represented remnants of old Smriti law. In any case however it is absurd to judge, from stray evidence of this character relating to very modern times, about the condition of societies about twenty centuries earlier.

It is hardly necessary at this late date to challenge the historical conclusions of Nelson on this head. If it were, they would be met by saying that the evidence adduced by the author

(*i*) Nelson, *Prospectus of a Scientific study of Hindu Law.* p. 44 and also at p. 161.

(*j*) Sir William Jones' Works Supplementary Volumes II p. 739.

(*k*) See Manu VIII. 49.

does not at all established what he seeks to prove. On the other hand it is quite apparent from internal evidence as well as from other authorities that Smriti law was the practical law administered at sometime in ancient India—no matter when ; and that the authors of commentaries and digests were not dilettantes engaged in building up elaborate aerial castles. The conclusion of Jolly on this head (*l*) will be endorsed by every one who has taken any nearly adequate view of Hindu law books. The evidence of epigraphic records (*m*), such as they are, also furnishes some independent corroboration of the theory that Smriti law was honoured by Hindu Kings. In literature too the trial scenes in Mricchakatika (*n*) and the Dhurtasamagama (*o*) show that in the main Smriti law was sought to be followed by kings in the times of their authors. But perhaps the question is altogether set at rest when we look at the vast body of non-jural customs of Hindu India of to-day (at any rate in northern India) which have not been affected by the political changes of history and which inspite of all aberrations and all subsequent influences are yet found to be based on an implicit acceptance of the authority of Smritis. That shows that Smriti law has been obeyed in India for ages even where there has not been any political sanctions for it. Is it a violent presumption then to assume that when the authority of Hindu Kings lent support to that law it had all the force and authority of positive law that a comparatively unorganised state of society in those days permitted?

I do not therefore make any further apology for founding my treatment of the subject on the Sanskrit works. I may say also, that in dealing with them I do not propose to tread on the thorny path of ancient Indian chronology which, so far as literature is concerned, is little more than a heap of guesses. It is happily not of much importance to us to arrive at any very accurate conclusions on the dates of the particular works we are dealing with. We are more concerned with what Ihering calls the "innere chronologie" of legal facts and this can be determined with reasonable certainty without our being anything like

---

(*l*) Jolly : Tagore Law Lectures p. 28.

(*m*) I refer to the land grants which strictly follow the form laid down in the Smritis for them. See Jolly Institutes of Vishnu p. 22 note. also Burnell. Elements of South Indian Paleography.

(*n*) A drama by Sudraka. A translation of trial scene with a synopsis of the plot by the present writer will be found in 16. C. W. N. p. iii.

(*o*) A farce referred to by Jolly at p. 68 of his Tagore Law Lectures. The Mudrarakshasa also furnishes some evidence of the authority of Smriti law.

equally sure whether our antiquities leads us back to two hundred or two thousand years before Christ or whether we must be contented with the ignominous nonage of a thousand years or less. It is comparatively easier to determine what were the real rudimentary conceptions of law in ancient India and also to trace the broad lines of development of most of these conceptions specially with the aid of studies in other system of ancient law which throw a great deal of light on the character of archaic law generally.

PART I.

§1. CONSTITUTION OF ANCIENT INDIAN SOCIETY.

The Smritis acquaint us with two different types of human habitation, the city (*nagara*) and the village (*grâma*). The administrative and constitutional law of the Smritis are concerned mainly with the cities where Kings reside, the Kings' courts administer justice and officers of the King maintain the peace and administer the revenues. Into the internal administration of the villages it gives us very little insight. The earliest information that we get about these *grâmas* would lead us to think that they were fortified dwellings governed by chieftains who do not seem to have been King's officers (*p*). The Smritis however give a picture of more peaceful times when the *grama* is placed in touch with the rest of the state by having a King's officer placed over it for purpose of police and revenue administration (*q*). The Smritis do not indicate that villages had much to do with military affairs ; for defence and aggression seem to have been in sole change of the central authority. Matters of private law also seem to have been outside the scope of the functions of the *gramadhipati*, for in the enumeration or description of tribunals for the decision of disputes we no where find a mention of the *gramadhipati* (*r*). In fact the village seems to have been a mere revenue and police division and did not necessarily correspond to the natural societies of men who exercised a great deal of influence over the lives of the people. The village does not appear to have been one social unit: on the one hand it was an aggregation of various societies within itself and on the other, the societies partly contained in the village might very well outstrip its boundaries and embrace several villages.

This may be more clearly elucidated by a consideration of the nature of Indian villages to-day which may throw a great deal

---

(*p*) Baden Powell, Indian Village Communities pp. 194—195.

(*q*) Manu VIII, 115 *et seq* ; Yajnavalkva I. 321 ; Apastamba II, 10, 26, 4. Vishnu II, 7 *et seq* ; There can be little doubt that the gramadhipati &c. of the Smrities were the Kings' officers. Baden Powell in saying that they were "hereditary headmen" (*op cit* p. 183) certainly goes beyond his evidence. For there is nothing in the Smritis to indicate that the office were hereditary or even that the officer was a "headman" in the sense of coming from amongst the villagers themselves.

(*r*) See Yajnavalkya II 30 ; Narada I, 7.

of light on the constitution as shadowed forth in the Smritis. I shall take as a type the village in Bengal. The Bengal village is generally regarded as a departure from the type of Indian villages mainly because the land-tenure here differs so remarkably from forms prevailing elsewhere in India and because Bengal society represents a more pronounced type of individualism than we find elsewhere (*s*). But I am afraid that certain peculiarities of land-tenure and village constitutions associated with it have been too readily assumed to represent the archaic type (*t*). On the other hand it might reasonably be held that land tenure was the one matter in which Indian society was most profoundly influenced by the Mahomedan rule. The opposition to Moslem aggression, where it was foiled on the political field, may have clung more tenaciously round the village and village lands in respect of which the villagers may have thus developed a greater degree of cohesion before the sovereign power could get at them. But apart from any such automatic change in proprietory ideas we have it as a definite historical fact that the Mahomedan rulers of India understood land tax more than anything else and that they brought with them ideas of land tenure which they impressed on the land laws of the country (*u*). Law of land-tenure would thus seem to be a most unreliable guide in the study of ancient society from the historical point of view.

There is on the other hand another side of the village life which has been very little, if at all, influenced by Mahomedan rule and has been only touched at the surface by a century and more of British rule. I refer of course to the body of non-jural customs which the Mitakshara distinguishes as *Achara* from *Vyavahara* or law. I include of course under achara all that is dealt with under *prayaschitta* in Mitakshara. Looked at from

(*s*) Baden Powell considers the village system as "decayed" in Bengal. That is scarcely the right word to use, for we do not know that any other village system ever existed in Bengal than the one that we find now. A truer view would be to hold that the Bengal village even now represents an archaic type not junior to the other system and traceable in the oldest Smritis. The elaboration of this position is not here possible, but the sketch which follows would make the position at least probable.

(*t*) See for instances Maine, Village *Communities* and Baden Powell. The *Indian Village Community* where almost exclusive attention is given to land tenures.

(*u*) If nothing else the superabundance of Arabic term in the land law would make this proposition highly probable. Compare the Arabic ideas of land tenure in Mr. Abdur Rahim's excellent work on *Mahomedan Jurisprudence* (Tagore Law Lectures) where the terms used may be compared with the expressions in daily used even to this day in land laws.

the point of view of these *acharas* we shall find the village even in Bengal disclosing elements which have their prototypes in ancient Smritis like those of Gautama, Apastamba, Baudhayana and Vasistha.

A Village in Modern Bengal.

Now looking at a Bengal village from this point of view it would be found to consist of a group of families belonging to various castes—which, it should be noted, do not, except in the case of the Brahman, correspond to the Smriti castes. A great fissure divides the clean castes who live in the village from the unclean ones who live apart, forming a *para* or "location" of their own. Within the clean castes again there is a broad division between the higher or *bhadralog* (literally, gentleman) castes including Brahmans, Vaidyas, Kayesthas, etc., and what are called "lower castes" who follow occupations which are deemed lowly by the higher castes.

Each caste forms a group which is not confined to its members within that village but includes members of the same caste in neighbouring villages which together constitute the sphere of the caste *samaj* (literally, society) within the ambit of which caste relations, such as marriage, interdining, etc., are permissible. Each family is also for many purposes a self-contained group and is affiliated to a larger group of families descended from a common stock (the *kula*). There is, besides these, a sort of a corporation of superior castes within the village which regulates all social matters, within certain limits, not only of the superior castes but also of the inferior castes though these have also caste societies of their own.

A position of pre-eminence is always reserved for the Brahman though this has been largely broken in upon by the pre-eminence of the Zemindar. Families have their own priests and, occasionally, there is but one village priest. There are usually one or more *Brahman pandits*, not priests, but persons learned in Sanskrit lore, to whom people appeal on all knotty questions of *âchara, prayaschitta* or worship and who are very often astrologers who know the *dies fasti* and the *dies nefasti* for religious functions and all little matters of every life such as entering a new house, ploughing or sowing the field, starting on a journey and so forth. There are also degraded Brahmans who assist in funerals at the crematorium. Besides these there are other functionaries who count in the economy of social life in the village, the barber, the washerman, the cobbler, the ferryman, the blacksmith, etc.

On matters of ritual and *achara* the villager of the clean castes (for whom a decent Brahman would officiate at the worship) is guided by rules of twofold origin. One set of these is derived from the Sruti, Smritis, Tantras, Puranas and other Sanskrit works of authority. On a great many matters small and great however he is governed by customs obtaining in the family, caste or *samaj*, which are known to the family priest, the family barber and pre-eminently to the old women of the family (*v*). These customs are outside the pale of Sanskrit law though not necessarily and certainly not openly, opposed to it. The unclean castes and have usages of their own. They have their own Brahmans who imitate the clean Brahmans but are almost always innocent of the dictates of Sanskrit religious law. The rituals at all important functions of their lives are generally equally elaborate with those of the clean castes, and, though somewhat original, are yet generally based on the imitation of the genuine Brahmin ritual. In theory they profess to be guided by the same sacred tradition as governs the superior castes but in practice they are ruled by a customary code of *achara* framed on the model of the Brahmanic but distinct from it. The result is that, though they do things forbidden in the Sastras, they never fail in proper respect to the Brahman.

In every caste therefore there is a large scope given to custom and usage. But while in Brahmans and the upper classes the custom is limited to a large extent by the sastras, the sphere of custom goes on enlarging as we go down the social scale till we reach the unclean castes with whom custom is practically everything and who never have occasion to confront the custom with the shastras.

Within the sphere of custom each man is governed, in respect of family rituals and usages and acts distinguished as *samajik* or social, partly by the village *samaj* and partly by the caste *samaj*. Among the lower castes the authority of their own *samaj* is to be a certain extent controlled by the pre-eminence of the upper classes.

On questions of *sastric* rules the village pandit is the authority to whom appeal is usually made. But on questions of more than ordinary interest appeal is made to centres of learning of note where a great many pandits congregate. They generally

(*v*) Cf. Apastamba II, 11, 29, 15.

unite in giving a *vyavastha* which generally concludes the matter unless it is overruled by the contrary *vyavastha* of a seat of learning of still greater eminence such as Vikrampore or Navadwip for instance.

I may notice here incidentally the authority which is generally exercised by the *Guru* over his disciples, who, under his authority from a sort of society marked off from the rest of the people. The *Guru* of Bengal is a *Tantric* institution but he has appropriated to himself the position which belonged to the *Guru* of the Smritis who was the teacher and spiritual guide of the pupil.

The most noticeable character of the society here depicted is the number of smaller societies (*w*) which go to build it up. The village is only one of such societies ; the family, the caste the *kula*, the community governed by the authority of a common college of learned men, that united by the authority of the *Guru* are some of the societies which go to build up the greater society which, given a political constitution would make a state.

Villages in the Smritis.

In more than one respect this picture of Bengal society of to-day reproduces features of ancient society as we find represented in old Smritis. The villages contemplated by these works were not tribal in their character in the sense in which Highland villages are tribal (*x*). They were peopled by men belonging to various castes who may be broadly divided into the clean, including what are called the Brahman Kshattriya, Vaisya and Sudra castes, and the unclean such as the Chandâla, Swapacha, Vyanga, Nishâda etc. (*y*) as also outcastes *abhisâstas* and *apa-*

(*w*) I use the term 'society' in the sense in which Stelzer and Mohl have used it, to signify, that is, any agregation of men with some permanent principle of association. I prefer to use the term without the qualifying epithet "metapolitical" which Steltzer prefixes to it, for we shall see that some of these societies have a good right to be called "antepolitical" rather than "metapolitical". See on this use of the term Korkunov ; General Theory of Law p. 328 *et seq.*

(*x*) This is perfectly consistent with their being tribal in the sense that the overlordship of the lands vested in the founders of the Aryan settlement which Baden Powell considers to be a characteristic of one type of villages. In every village, whether founded by a clan or by a chance association of men, there was always a miscellaneous population belonging to various castes and following various occupations more or less rigorously associated with their respective castes.

(*y*) Chandalas are always contemplated as residing out of the villages see Apastamba 1, 3, 9, 15, and 19. The term बाह्याः in the last Sutra, *pâtras* (z) who live apart from the main village and whom it is an impurity to touch. Washermen, dancers, (châranas) and some other classes of a like character are mentioned with contempt but it is not clear whether they lived in the village or out of it. The unclean castes lived in locations and were outside the pale of sacred law and formed communities who governed themselves like outcastes (a).

Within the clean castes there was a distinction between Arya or Dwija and Sudra, the upper classes following respectable callings and the lower whose occupations were looked upon as lowly. Sudras were not slaves but evidently freemen and not necessarily servants of the Aryas (b) ; but they appear to have followed occupations which the Arya disdained. At the same time they were within the pale of sacred law and it was not pollution to touch a Sudra (c). Like the modern Bengal society the ancient society depicted in the Smritis was an aggregate of many minor societies. The family and the gens (*Kula*) were very early societies which we can trace in the Vedic literature. In the Grihya Sutras we are introduced to the Sâkha which we can trace all through subsequent literature (d). This *sâkha* was a religious society of men who accepted the same set of vedic texts and same ceremonials in respect of all of which differences had grown up. Sâkhas were larger societies which included various *charanas* representing the sub-groups founded on further divergences in custom and possibly associated with the parishads of the

---

which evidently implies residence out of the village, has been interpreted by Haradatta as including Ugras, Nishâdas, etc. Bühler's translation as "outcastes" is scarcely correct, for it implies men who have been deprived of their caste status. Gautama XVI, 19 ; Manu X 51. The word बाह्या : is very often used for these castes, see Manu X, 29, 30.

(z) See Apastamba I, 10, 29, 8 ; Baudhâyana II, 1, 2, 18.

(a) Gautama IV 25. They were धर्महीना: but they could have quasi-religious institutions amongst them and certainly had jural relations according to their own customs. Apastamba I, 10, 29, 8. See Part II §8.

(b) See for instance Baudhâyana I. 5, 10, 20 where he obviously implies that these were sudras who were not servants. Lawful occupations for sudras other than service are recognised in many places. See on this Baden Powell *op cit* p. 191 *et seq*. Manu X, 99 ; Gautama X 60. Gautama's text seems to indicate that the position of a sudra was analogus to that of a client in Roman law rather than to that of a slave or servant. Kautilya mentions कारुकुशीलवकर्म as functions of Sudras. *Arthasastra* p.7.

(c) On the contrary Sudras were permitted to cook food for the Vaiswadeva sacrifice. Apastamba II, 2, 3, 4.

(d) See Max Muller, History of Ancient Sanskrit Literature p. 50—52.

Smritis (*e*). The pupils of the same teacher and their pupils together constituted a society (*vidyâvamsa*) which had a strong element of cohesion and in some cases inherited to one another Besides these there were the village and associations of fellow castemen and persons following the same avocation. Each of these societies had a large measure of individuality and independence and were often the judges and law givers of the men belonging to the community (*f*).

Every village was expected to have in or near it one or more srotriyas or men well versed in sacred learning who were appealed to for guidance on all questions of life having a religious or quasi-religious bearing. A number of villages together would habitually refer more important matters to a seat of learning where an assembly of learned men (Parishad) existed (*g*).

THE CASTE SYSTEM.

The caste system would appear to be a most important feature of the society in the times of the Smritis. It would be wrong however to take the caste scheme of the Smritis as representing the actual divisions and the only actual divisions of society at all times. To start with, it was a theory embodying the broad classification of men in society which did not necessarily imply that each of these classes was a homogeneous caste. The Brahmans whom we find from the outset divided into various sâkhas and kulas and also parted from one another by territorial boundaries were the most homogeneous class and answered to the description of a caste. The Kshattriyas are more uncertain in character and appear to have represented really different castes in different states—the only element of likeness in them being their kinship with the King. The Vaisya was the name not of a caste but of the entire body of respectable classes who are differentiated from the privileged classes on the one hand and the servile class on the other (*h*).

Indeed, it would seem that the Indian people fell into natural groups or classes according to differences of occupation, descent, race or territory. These classes must naturally have been many,

(*e*) See post. Part II §3.

(*f*) See Gautama VI 21, Yajnavalkya II, 30 ; Narada 1, 7. Does Vasistha XVI, 15 also indicate the same rule ? On the law making functions of societies see Manu VIII 219—20 Yajn II 186, 192.

(*g*) See post Part II §3.

(*h*) See Muir Ancient Sanskrit Texts p. 292 ; Baden Powell *op cit* p. 186.

with greater or less element of cohesion amongst them. The caste theory, which, whether it dates back to the Rig Veda or not (*i*) was assuredly one of great antiquity, singled out from among these various classes some more salient principles of classification; it looked upon the people as divided into four broad classes and sought to give the general characteristic functions of each class. As the leading classes in society became more and more identified with the theory, castes become more and more rigid, though it would be wrong to say that the actual divisions ever corresponded to the simple division into four classes. The correspondence between the theory and fact was secured by the twofold process of approximation I have adverted to above. On the one hand the theory itself was amplified and on the other the existing classifications in society tended to throw themselves into line with the theoretical classification.

The first division of men was into the respectable and the servile. And from the respectable classes again were isolated two privileged classes who enjoyed a special measure of pre-eminence in society. From the earliest times the Aryan people appear to have had a body of men devoted to religious meditation and worship who were looked upon with great veneration. The Druids of Britain, the Brehons of Ireland, the Magi of Persia, and the Pontiffs of Rome represent these primitive meditators who had a monopoly of spiritual learing. Of such a class we also find traces in Babylonian tradition referred to the Kassites who certainly had a large element of Aryan culture amongst them and may have, at least, borrowed this institution from them (*j*). This

---

(*i*) See on the controversy on this subject Muir *op·cit* p. 290 et seq.

(*j*) "There undisturbed and unmolested they (the Cushite islanders) could develop a certain spirit of abstract speculation. They were great star-gazers and calculators. Thoughts of heavenly things occupied them much ; they worked out a religion beautiful in many ways ; *their priests dwelt in communities or colleges*, probably one in every island, and spent their time not only in *scientific study and religious contemplation* but *also in the more practical art of government*, for there do not appear as yet to have been any kings amongst them". *Chaldea (Story of Nations* series) p. 191. The whole description and specially the portions I have italicised strongly remind one of the Brahman of ancient India. On the strong infusion of Aryan culture and Aryan population amongst Kassites see J. Kennedy : *Prehistoric Aryans and the Kings of Mitani*. J. R. A. S. 1909 p. 1313. The Kassites, says Kennedy, "were not Aryans though coming from Media they might be confounded with Medes ; probably they were as much mixed a multitude as that which followed Cyrus". Berosus' account of this onfall of Kassites as that of Medes however seems to render the probability of their being Aryans after all not quite negligible.

ancient body of men devoted to religious pursuits as also to the art of Government were undoubtedly as much pre-eminent in India at the time of the Purusha Sukta as the Druids were in Britain.

The other privileged class was one whose claim to pre-eminence was founded on their kinship or affinity with the king and their military leadership. The tendency of descendants and relations of kings to form a class by themselves is nothing unusual, and is traceable in all societies from the royal princes of modern Europe to the thakurs of our Native States. Add to this the further element of cohesion in the "noble art of war" which almost made the knights of the middle ages into a caste and the pre-eminence of this class in fact would be seen to be only natural (*k*). The pre-eminence of the royal caste was primarily based on their association with the king who was pre-eminently the Kshattra (*l*). War was their special occupation, but we hear to Kshattriyas only as captains and never as privates. It would seem that the rank and file was drawn from the Sudras and even other classes and military occupation in itself did not make a man a Kshattriya.

Excluding these privileged classes the people were divided into born masters and those born to serve. Such was the basis upon which the caste theory of the Purusha Sukta was based. This classification had such an element of reasonableness about it that it is nothing surprising that the authors of the theory looked upon it as given by eternal law. In fact Plato in his effort at a rational classification of men in an ideal society arrived at a division not much dissimilar to this (*m*). The philosophical Guardians of Plato with their rigorous training and privileges bear remarkable

---

(*k*) It may be however that the royal race in various states into which the Aryan settlement was divided did not really form a homogeneous caste. And it may be that revolutions affected the privileged position of quandam khattriyas. At any rate it is a significant fact that there is no Kshattriya caste named as such in India to-day. There are no doubt castes claiming the privileges of Kshattriyas but they are not called Kshattriyas.

(*l*) The literal meaning of *Kshattra* is powerful. In the Vedas it is an epithet of Divinity. *Kshathra* in the Zend Avesta means the power of God. In Babylon the King as high priest was called *khattesi*. Though linguistic arguments' are slippery, one is here tempted to draw one, which may support the derivation of the pre-eminence of the kshattriya from the divine power represented in the king.

(*m*) Plato : Republic Books II—IV. So also King Alfred, "Unless there are priests, soldiers and workmen—*gebedmen, fyrdmen* and *weorcmen*—no king can show his craft"' Seebohm ; *English Village Community* 3rd Ed. p. 133. cited by Baden Powell p. 186.

analogies to the Brahman, the Auxiliaries are near kindred to the common Kshattriya and the Vis and the Artisans who form the residuary population are alike devoted to industial and commercial pursuits. The Indian theory however goes further than Plato in conceiving with Aristotle (*n*) that there were some men who were born to serve and others who were born to be served. The exclusive attention given to the hereditary principle is a point of difference between Greek and Indian theories, but even in Greece the dramatist stands out strongly for the ancient principle of heredity when he makes Helen say,

"Who should presume to term me serf
The offspring of a twofold stock divine" (*o*).

The very naturalness and simplicity of this fourfold classification ought to prepare us to believe that it never corresponded completely with the natural classes existing in society (*p*) and we find that though the Brahmans and to some extent the Kshattriyas were more or less homogeneous classes, Vaisya and Sudra were names not for single castes but for a multitude of different classes. Within those who had been thus classed there were a number of classes who had all the qualities which would go to make a caste. There were, besides, communities whom the Sudras himself would look down upon such as the Chandalas, Nishâdas, Swapâks &c. There appear also to have been men who formed classes with a sufficient degree of cohesion amongst themselves and bore definite class names who would, nevertheless, not wholly answer to the description of any one of the four Varnas.

It was to bridge this gulf between fact and theory that the theory of *varnasankara* was developed and made its appearance in the Smritis. In the earlier Smritis caste mixture is mentioned but the list of mixed castes was comparatively meagre. They grow in number however as the theory approximates more to fact and embraces a larger and larger number of castes and in the encyclopedæic work of Manu it rises to the respectable figure of

---

(*n*) Aristotle: *Politics* (Welldon's translation p. 8—16.

(*o*) Quoted by Aristotle (Welldon's translation) p. 15 another remarkable coincidence between the Indian and Greek point of view is that Plato like the author of the Purusha Sukta seeks to maintain the preeminence of his Guardians by a story about their mystic origin. *Republic* (Trans. in the Golden Treasury series) pp. 112—113.

(*p*) It is noticeable however that the Persians had practically the same classification of people omitting the Sudras. Their view represents the theoretical classification of Aryans, prior to the later developments that we find in the Indian law. See *Zend Avesta*, Darmesteter's translation Vol. II p. 201 Farvardin Yast 88.

forty-four (*q*). Other devices by which aberrations from the caste theory are explained are the hypotheses of castes having lost their achara or persons not having received their initiation according to the holy law. Castes and peoples of countries, otherwise estimable, who were found not to follow the Aryan sacred customs were classed as Vrishalas and Vrâtyas.

I have indulged in this somewhat long digression on the nature of the Smriti theory of caste because I think it necessary to understand it properly in order to appreciate the true character of ancient Indian society, in the atmosphere of which the Dharmasastras were framed, and to appreciate the exact scope of the holy Hindu law.

Societies in Ancient Indian States.

Returning now to the picture of ancient Indian society we find that men were here naturally understood to belong to one or more groups or societies which exercised a direct control over their conduct with some minuteness. Some of these societies must have been comparatively late products, for, with the growth of civilisation, people naturally discover principles of association unknown to a more primitive state. But at the same time some of these societies must have belonged to the most primitive times that we can think of . The family and the kula are undoubtedly more primitive organisations than the State. It would be rash also to say that religious fraternity did not reach back to an earlier date than the political association called a state. A more proper view of society would be to look upon an ancient state like one of the Hindus as an aggregate of several societies, embodying

(*p*) I can here give but a bare outline of the conclusions at which I have arrived on the caste theory without attempting any elaborate justification. That the varnasankara theory is a mere theory brought in to remove the inadequacy of the theory of varnas would appear from several facts. Some arguments would be found in R. C. Dutt's *Ancient India.* Besides it should be noted the tradition about mixed marriages that we have in the Mahabharata and the Vedas is wholly against the Smriti theory of Varnasankara. Then again the Smritis themselves are not quite unanimous about the exact mixture which gives rise to any of the Sankara castes. Further, we know the principle upon which this classification was based. Where you have a definite homogeneous class following occupations which partake of the character of two different castes as laid down in the shâastras this class is put down as a hybrid of the two primary castes. For an enumeration of the mixed castes and Vrâtyas and Vrishalas see Manu X, 8 et seq with which compare Gautama IV 16 et seq ;Baudhâyana II, 2, 3 Vasistha XVII. Vishnu XVI, Yajnavalkya I 91 et seq.

different principles of association, loosely knit together by the military principle into a rudimentary State. In the earliest Smritis we find the authority of the State as represented by the king already largely consolidated but at the same time the other societies enjoy a position of independence to a very great extent. In the Grihya Sutras we find the authority of the society of *Desa*, *jati* and *kula* fully recognised in respect of *âchara*. The Sakha also is already recognised as exercising a paramount authority in respect of rituals (*r*). Gautama in his Dharma Sutras enjoins the king to administer justice according to the customs of *desa*, *jati* and *kula* (*s*) ; according to the dictates of learned Brahmans (*t*) who are the constituted heads of religious society competent to lay down the holy law (*u*) ; and according to the decisions of husbandmen, traders, herdsmen, money-lenders and artisans in respect of affairs touching them (*v*).

Here in these works we find the authority of the military principle as embodied in the king almost in its cradle and we watch it growing with time till we find in Manu that the king is authorised to legislate (*w*). While in the earlier Smritis the duty of the king to regard these various societies is imperative, in Manu and Yajnvalkya it almost sinks to a recommendation and a matter of grace, except of course in the matter of the religious societies represented by the Brahman and the Parishad.

We cannot therefore be far wrong in assuming that these various societies, each representing a different principle or social force operating in society, grew up more or less independently, contemporaneously with the military organisation or at any rate before the military organisation had grown into the homogeneous state (*x*). The subsequent history of Indo-Aryan society was a

(*r*) See Max Müller : *History of Ancient Sanskrit Literature* p. 50—52.

(*s*) Gautama XI, 20, Apastamba II, 6, 15, 1 ; Vasistha XIX, 7. Manu VII 41 ;

(*t*) Gautama XI, 25 ;

(*u*) Vasistha I, 401 ; Gautama XXVIII 50 ; Baudhâyana I 1, 1, 13 et seq.

(*v*) Gautama XI 21.

(*w*) Manu VII 13 ; Yaju. II, 186 also assumes such powers.

(*x*) Hindu society of the Smritis illustrates in fact the dictum of Bryce that "Physical force had plenty of scope in the strife of clan or cities, or (somewhat later) of frictions with one other ; but in building up the clan or city it was hardly needed." "In primitive societies" he says "three forces other than fear have been extremely powerful, the reverence for ancient lineage, the instinctive deference to any person of marked gifts, (with the disposition to deem those gifts supernatural) and

history of the integration of these various principles under a ruling one and the subordination of all societies to the one representing the ruling idea. This ruling idea was furnished by the integration of the military with the religious principles in a manner which gave to the military principle itself a secondary position.

While thus the religious military society dominated the whole development in the process of the integration of society the other societies were not altogether obliterated, but rather sought to be welded into an organic whole. In a primitive state a man might belong to two or more societies which grew up in comparative isolation from one another without any serious conflict of authority. But after a certain stage of progress is reached the different societies might come into conflict and occasion would arise for a delimitation of their spheres of influence. In the process of adjustment by which a limitation of the sphere of each society was reached, some must needs be subordinated to others and the whole series placed under the governing authority of one, in order that organic life of society may be possible. In this state each subordinate society has a limited sphere within which it has authority. This is the state to which we find ancient Indian society approximating in Manu and Yajnavalkya.

To the primitive societies which must have been already existing the caste theory furnished another principle of cohesion. It had really the effect of throwing a great number of societies into some broader groups. These larger groups thus became new societies which began to exercise authority over the minor societies and over individuals belonging to them.

The religious society which, in concert with the military, gained an ascendancy over the others was ruled, of course, by the Brahmans. The practical authority in respect of the religious law was vested in the Parishads and only in a subordinate degree in any learned Brahman.

KINGSHIP.

At the top of the various societies we find the King, a joint offshoot of the military and the religious principles. The king is always an exalted personage who represents more or less of

---

the associative tendency which unites the members of a group or tribe so closely together that the practice of joint action supersedes individual choice. These forces have imprinted the habit of obedience so deeply upon the early communities that it became a tradition moulding the minds of succeeding generations."

Bryce: *Studies in History and Jurisprudence*, II 21.

divine power, but not sufficiently to be able to displace the authority of the Brahmans the constituted Guardians of society. In him are vested the command of the military, the headship of the revenue and police functions, guardianship of infants and other functions of a like character. Justice is administered by him or a minister of his, in later Smritis, with the assistance of learned assessors (*y*).

With the elaborate executive machinery which he controlled we are not very much concerned. But his judicial functions would deserve some consideration.

The King's courts naturally engross a great deal of the attention of Smriti writers. Elaborate rules of procedure are found developed in Smritis which are marked by such practical common sense that they leave little doubt that Kings sought to observe them in the practical administration of justice. These rules of procedure are however obviously meant to apply only to the King's courts. Besides these there were other tribunals which undoubtedly exercised considerable authority, at any rate, out of the city. A gâtha quoted by Asahâya (*z*), which is obviously very old, clearly shows that there were tribunals in the villages from whose decision you could appeal to the city. Yajnavalkya and Narada give us a fuller list of tribunals. These consist, according to them, of the Kula or gens, the srenis or societies, the puga or gana or the assembly of the people (of a village or town) the courts presided over by the King's judges and, lastly, the King himself (*a*). The last two sat obviously in cities and were regular courts. For the

(*y*) For the functions of the King See Gautama X 7—48 ; XI ; XIII, 26 ; Apastamba II, 7, 12 ; II, 10, 14 ; II, 11, 1—4 ; II, 25, 1—29, Vasistha I, 41—43 ; XVI 2—9 ; 21—26 ; XIX ; Baudhayana 1, 18—19, Manu VII ; Yajnavalkya I 301—368, Vishnu II.

(*z*) Commentary Narada I, 11.

ग्रामे दृष्टः पुरे याति पुरे दृष्टस्तु राजनि ।
राज्ञा दृष्टः कुदृष्टो वा नास्ति पौनर्भवो विधिः ॥

(*a*) Narada I, 7 ; Yajnavalkya II 30.

कुलानि श्रेणयश्चैव गणाश्चाधिकृतो नृपः
प्रतिष्ठा व्यवहाराणां पूर्व्वेभ्यस्तूत्तरोत्तरम् ॥

Narada.

Yajnavalkya gives :—

नृपेणाधिकृताः पूगाः श्रेणयोऽथ कुलानि च ।
पूर्व्वं पूर्व्वं गुरु ज्ञेयं व्यवहारविधौ नृणाम् ॥

Asahâya's explanation of the terms differs from that in the Mitâksharâ. I follow the latter which is preferable.

rest, it was merely an adjudication by a society of disputes between its members subject to an appeal to (or rather retrial by) the higher authority of a wider society.

It is usual to say that the association of Kingship with the administration of justice is the primary fact in juristic history. Sir Henry Maine finds in this association the whole historical foundation of law. This view, so plausible in itself, and supported, as it is, by authorities in the Bible and in Homer, labours under a serious defect however in not allowing for difference in the types of civilisation and social organisation. Kingship is primarily an institution representative of the military principle (*b*) and this obtains in different degrees of ascendancy in different primitive societies. In Aryan societies, for instance, it never obtained the degree of ascendancy which it had amongst the Semites and Mongolians (*c*). And, the military principle or the military society was not the only nor the earliest society in ancient communities (*d*). We have seen that there must have been other societies in India growing side by side with the military; amongst these morality and religion must have arisen before the military society organised itself into a state. The idea of justice of some sort must have existed in these antepolitical societies and they must have been called upon, so soon as the first acute stage of self-helf was past, to decide between the conflicting claims of the members of that society long before the military captain thought of interfering in the private affairs of the members of the society. Some sort of gentile arbitration, and, when other societies grew upon the model of the gens, arbitration by members of that society, must have existed before judicial authority was centralised in the King. The recognition of such arbitrations in the late works of Narada and Yajnavalkya is a remnant of the old times and not a new delegation of power. A similar state of affairs in archaic society in Rome and amongst the Germanic races has been noticed by scholars. Everywhere we find the gentile organisation as a tribunal for the decision of disputes between its members and the regulator of more important juristic and social acts such as adoption or testament. We find also the development of other societies on the model of the gens to which similar rights are attached, in the Hundred in England, the Curiæ in Rome as in the Pugas and Srenis in India. Instances

(*b*) Ihering: Geist der Römishen Rechts (6th Ed.) I, 178.

(*c*) Miraglia: Comparative Legal Philosophy, Translation by John Lisle p. 120.

(*d*) Ihering, loc cit.

might be multiplied but these show sufficiently the ancient character of the gentile tribal and village government an essential part of which was the adjudication of disputes by the society to which a man belonged,—an idea which survives in the notable provision of the Magna Charta recognising the right of the people to be judged by their peers. That is a trait of early society everywhere and the assumption of judicial authority by the king would in ancient society be met with the same resentment as drove the barons to extort this admission from an erring king (*e*).

The Judicial authority of the King presupposes a toning down of military activities so that the king might have time to look to his people. When such a stage was reached, the king was found in a position of pre-eminence commanding the obedience of people to an unusual degree. To such a man all power in the society would naturally tend to gravitate. But it seems likely that his judicial authority in private law owed its origin to his control over the public peace which inevitably followed his military authority. The history of the expansion of the jurisdiction of the King's court in England is an instructive illustration of the way in which judicial authority may have been drawn to the king in pre-historic times. The fictitious allegations contained in the phrases *contra pacem* and *vi et armis* in the old writ of trespass were put in to give jurisdiction to the King's judges by taking out the cases from the jurisdiction of the popular courts. That seems to indicate that first judicial functions of the king were called forth for the purpose of maintaining peace, and after that, the fiction of the peace being involved was evoked to extend the jurisdiction so as to supplant the people's courts.

The *Legis Actio Sacramento* of Rome which has been looked upon by scholars as a dramatic representation of the act of a Roman king interfering with a private quarrel also suggests the same conclusion. For the Praetor or the King interfered in this *Legis Actio* only when both parties had gone through the symbolism of a preparation to fight over something. The king could only interfere in a quarrel if the peace was at stake and it was this tradition which was kept up by this fictitious preparation to fight. This was the only foundation for the authority of the king to interfere and, like the *contra pacem* and *vi et armis* of the old English writs, was kept up to give jurisdiction to the king. It is significant also that in Rome the dispute was invariably referred

(*e*) Apastamba II, 11, 29, 5 contemplates private persons as judges *par excellence*. Gautama also contemplates other judges than the King XIII, 26 ; also Baudhayana I, 10, 19, 8.

to the arbitration of a private person, so great was the jealousy of people to the king's affecting to judge between them, a distrust which was obviously referrible to his possession of the imperium—a power of military origin.

In Indian tradition too we do not notice the adjudication of civil disputes between persons referred to as an important function of the King and the King's judicial function is rarely referred to in the general enumeration of his duties. But the maintenance of peace and security, the prevention of *sâhasa* or violent offences and the infliction of punishment figure very prominently from the first to last among his functions (*f*). We find scanty references to the judicial functions of the king in Gautama and Apastamba and Gautama requires him to take the decisions of learned men and of tradesmen, artisans, etc., in the decision of disputes. As we come to later times we find this branch of the law expanding and an elaborate law of procedure for the King's courts is expounded in Manu, Narada and Yajnavalkya.

In Manu, Narada and Yajnavalkya we find kingship in the zenith of power. The autonomous village and minor societies appear to have considerably dwindled in authority and in Yajnavalkya are clearly supervised by leaders appointed by the King ; judicial power of the king original and appellate has grown to enormous proportions and popular tribunals reduced to a position of inferiority, exercising their functions by sufferance and subject to correction by the king. All the power that there is in the State centres round the king and the old societies retained a part of their old authority by a sort of delegation.

But all the time that the King's power was growing, limitations of a constitutional character were closing round him. In the older Smritis, if the power of the King is not quite as extensive as in Manu, Yajnavalkya and Narada, the King was subject to no constitutional restraints in the exercise of his functions (*g*).

(*f*) Gautama X & XI ; Apastamba II, 5, 11, 1, where a king is mentioned as punishing crimes. In the more elaborate enumerations in the *Râjadharmaprakarana* of Manu VII and Yajnavalkya (I, 301—368) the king is of course mentioned as looking after vyarahara but by far the more important function is protecting people from crimes. See e.g. Yajnavalkya 1. 336, Megasthenes (Fr. XXVII ed. Schwanbeck) says that in his time kings were much occupied with criminal cases but little with civil suits.

(*g*) In none of the extant sutra Smritis do we find any mention of the King's *sabhâ* and the king is called upon to do all sorts of work himself. Megasthenes too does not seem to have noticed the *sâbhâ* (Frag. XXVII Ed. Schwanbeck) Kautilya in his Arthasastra (III 57—58 ; p. 147 Mysore Ed.) does not mention the King's *sabhâ*.

But the king in Manu, Yajnavalkya and Narada can only transact public business in his General Council (*h*), though for confidential matters be had a sort of Privy Council of Ministers. In the General Council he was assisted by a body of constituted advisers—men who were noted for their learning and attainments—and by the royal priest (*i*) and the Prâdvivâk who held a position of great eminence. Besides these constitutional advisers there were invited to the council one of more unattached savants (*j*) who gave their advice, without the responsibility however which attached to the advice of councillors. His confidential advisers were ministers, preferably Brahmans (*k*), but always learned in law, politics, logic and the usual arts and sciences. Amongst these the Pradvivak mentioned by Narada is the chief Judicial officer (*l*). The authority of the sacred law as represented by the Brahman advisers and ministers of the king had altogether appropriated all the effective functions of the King by the time when the King's power had grown to the extent that we find in Manu or Yajnavalkya.

As I have just observed, the King's *sabhâ* is an institution which, in the precise form which it took in the metrical Smritis, did not exist at the time of the older works. But the germs of it we find in the dicta of Gautama and Apastamba requiring the king to administer justice according to sacred law and by referring all questions of difficulty to learned Brahmans and Parishads (*m*). The constant need for reference to learned persons

---

(*h*) Manu VIII 1 Yajnavalkya II 1 et seq. Narada I, 15. Vishnu III 33 Katyayana quoted in Mitakshara under Yajn. II, 2.

सप्राड्विवाक् सामात्य: सब्राह्मण पुरोहित: । सभ्यैर्भी प्रेक्षको राजा स्वर्गे तिष्ठति धार्मिक: ।

(*i*) Katyayana *above*, Yajn I, 313.

(*j*) Yajnavalkya II 2 and Mitakshara thereunder.

(*k*) Katyayana cited in Mitakshara II 3 ; Manu VIII I, 13.

(*l*) Of this officer we do not hear in any work earlier than Katyayana above and Narada (1 25). Manu (VIII 9) and Yajnavalkya (II, 3) no doubt refer to the appointment by the king of a learned Brahman to act in his place as judge when he has not time to attend to judicial business, but this Brahman is not a permanent officer. In Narada and Katyayana we find him however not only as a permanent officer under the name Pradvivak but also as having authority even in the presence of the king. Nay more the king is exhorted to do justice "in accordance with the opinion of the Pradvivak"— प्राड्विवाकमतेस्थित । —This clearly implies that in Narada's time the King had ceased to exercise any judicial functions and simply gave his formal authority to the acts of his chief judge much in the same way as the King in England does to the decisions of the Judicial Committee of the Privy Council.

(*m*) Gautama XI 25.

may have gradually led to the attachment to the court of a more or less permanent body of learned men who gradually grew into an institution. It may be just possible that the old Vedic Parishad of the clan may have thus associated itself with the King's sabha, but at any rate the sabha thus formed did answer to the description of Parishads in the Smritis and carried with it all the authority which the sacred books would attribute to the Parishad.

Another important institution of ancient Indian society was the Parishad whose existence can be traced back to the Vedic times and which exerted a great influence in making and moulding Hindu law in its earlier stages. A consideration of the nature history and authority of this institution I shall however postpone for the present.

§2. Social Ends in Ancient India.

I have mentioned before that in the moulding of Hindu society the religious element played a most important part Indeed it would be no exaggeration to say that all through its history Hindu society was wholly dominated by the religious idea. That is a characteristic of all primitive societies which are, in Compte's words, in the theological stage of civilization. It is important to note however that the religious idea in ancient Indian society is to be distinguished from the ideas associated with barbarism in that, in Hindu society, the primitive religious belief had yielded place to a philosophy of life which maintained and prolonged the primitive religious constitution of society only under a deeper ruling thought.

It would not be true to say that this vast continent had but one system of philosophy and one even course of history of culture. But there are a few characteristics which may be traced in all stages of Indian civilization more or less. Life was never, with the Indian, an end in itself. It was always looked upon as a means for the attainment of definite ends. The end too was uniformly some form of Beatitude or self-realisation. This does not mean that renunciation was anything like a universal rule or that the doctrine of Maya was more than the opinion of a school, albeit a very important school, of thought. All systems of philosophy and popular thought however agree in prescribing a course for the ultimate attainment of Bliss even through the worldly life by following the path of Dharma. The ideal worked out in the Smritis is clearly the attainment of regious merit by the pursuit of conduct prescribed by Dharma. Authors like Manu and Yajnavalkya no doubt occasionally refer to renunciation and

Yoga but that is not the concern of Dharmasastras which have to deal with common men following the common code of dharma. As the Mitakshara puts it, for the Yogi these rules are of no avail (*n*).

All schools of thought agree in holding that the world is not a fortuitous concourse of atoms, that nothing in fact happens by chance. Everything that there is has been brought into being by some necessary process and is moulded by some ultimate purpose, viz., to realise Dharma and ultimately to aid in the emancipation of men. Society, particularly, was looked upon as a Divine or rather eternal organisation founded and held together by Dharma.

The end of society was therefore the promotion of Dharma or the moral order of the Universe. All law was viewed as subsumed under that ruling conception. Law was therefore not a matter to be made or moulded by human hands. It is eternally ordained and imbedded in the constitution of society and capable of ascertainment partly by revelation and partly by enquiry, in a spirit of reverence, into the nature of Dharma.

The result of this was the development of a comprehensive idea of law which is the dream and perhaps the despair of the sociological school of modern philosophical jurists. It was this which prevented the strictly legal portion of Hindu laws from being totally divorced from the whole body of normative rules with which it is intimately associated, in spite of the important development and specialisation which Vyavahara had in the hands of later jurists. From the first to the last, Hindu law books hold a rule of conduct equally sacred no matter whether it relates to the every day duties of a householder or to broad questions of state or social status. A violation of that rule would not be a mere breach of a duty of prudence or of a private right leading to legal results, but, over and above such results, there would be *adharma* or outrage to *dharma* with consequences in the Hereafter which would have to be redressed, no matter whether by *danda*, self-infliction, pravaschitta or reparation, which are all different ways of dharma adjusting itself. The modes of redress and the sources from which it came were, to the ancient Hindu jurists, of little moment ; they did not seek a principle of differentiation in these. They revelled rather in the principle of unity embodied in the conception of *Dharma*.

The king or the Judge was under the obligation to adjudge

(*n*) Mitakshara under Yajn. I, 8,

the punishment or compel the performance of prayaschitta. If for weakness or wickedness the king failed to do so, he himself would incur sin (*o*), the sin of the wrongdoer would be divided between the persons responsible for the failure of justice (*p*).

The matter which was looked upon by Hindu law-givers as of far greater importance than anything else was the maintenance of the social order, which was itself looked upon as a matter of eternal ordination. Caste is looked upon as an integral part of the social order and the king is enjoined over and over again to maintain the *varnas* and *asramas* as a primary duty more binding than doing justice. From what has been said before about the nature of caste such an attitude towards it would seem to be quite natural and we find an echo of the same feeling in Plato when he identifies justice with the principle which kept the several classes in their proper places.

These in brief are the fundamental principles of the Hindu social philosophy and their social ends and ideals as worked out in the Smritis and vouched for, not only by their law and philosophy, but by the whole range of Sanskrit literature in all its spheres. It was the ascendancy of these principles and ideals that gave to the Brahman his position of pre-eminence in society and maintained him there from the earliest to the latest period of Hindu history. For the Brahman as understood by the Smritis was the embodiment of the religious principle and his was a life devoted from birth to death to the cause of dharma.

There is a tendency in some European writers to discount the claims of Brahmans and of the so-called Brahmanism to the antiquity and universality that are claimed for them. Brahmanism, it is said, was a late growth and was imposed at a comparatively late date on the simple and secular law to which the esoteric ideas of Smriti were foreign. Some even go further and claim that the religious-philosophical principles underlying Sanskrit law had no relation to life in ancient India and do not enter into the actual life of the people to-day. If by all this they mean that there is and always was a large body of men to whom the general rules and principles of law embodied in the Smritis were not applicable, they are undoubtedly right and as I shall show in the sequel they have excellent authority for that view in the Smritis themselves (*q*). The smritis themselves contemplate the government of

(*o*) Yajn I 337.

(*p*) Manu VIII, 18 See also VIII, 12, 14.

(*p*) See post. Part II §8.

vast populations by their customs alone, and the fact that they are so governed would not derogate from the general authority and antiquity of Smritis. But if they mean that the Smriti law and the ideas it stands for was an improvement on the practical law of the people, junior in date to the old customary law and that the authority of the Brahman was a new-fangled idea of the degenerate days of Hindu society they are certainly wrong.

In the first place it is perfectly clear that the Brahman and the religious and contemplative men from whom they were descended were never otherwise then predominant in Aryan society. I have already referred to the evidences indicating the predominance of the religious class amongst Aryans. In India, at the furthest limits to which her literature leads us we find the Rishis placed in a position of undoubted pre-eminence of which even kings like Viswamitra were jealous. Whether we agree with Dr. Haug that the Brahman as a caste existed in the days of the Rig Veda or not, we can say with perfect assurance that at any rate the fererunners of the Brahman caste were placed at the top of society. In the Brahmanas the position of the Brahman caste is well assured. The Upanishads no doubt deal very often with the learning and spiritual pre-eminence of Kshattriyas but even in the very passages where these are extolled we can find the pre-eminence of the Brahman in society recognised. King Janaka's attitude towards the Brahman Yâjnavalkya is one of considerable reverence. Ajatasatru speaks in a tone of unmistakeable deference when he addresses Svetaketu, the Brahmin scholar whom he was to teach. Coming to later times we find in the Kalpa Sutras, in the Mahabharata and the Ramayana, the Smritis and the Puranas the position of the Brahman thoroughly well assured. In the present day society his pre-eminence, though often unaccompanied by the equipments with which it was associated in ancient times, is, if possible, greater still. The Brahman then was not a late development but an institution which was a part and parcel of the Hindu society at all ages.

In the second place the notion that the ideas of the so-called Brahmanism were a mushroom growth on the simple organism of archaic law is not only unsupported by history but is opposed to all that we know of ancient society and ancient law. Hindu society even up to this date is thoroughly saturated with these ideas. The testimony of the entire literature of the Hindu races is all in favour of the antiquity and universality of these ideas. It seems bold indeed to brush aside this one-sided evidence in favour of theories based upon an imperfect acquaintance with the life, convictions and habits of the people of to-day, and to base on it a theory of society ages ago before the numerous cataclysms of Indian history had happened. It is true that the literature belonged to the upper ten of society. But are there not a thousand and one ways in which ideas now held by the upper classes filter down to the lower strata and become the common property of the whole race? And do not the learned men of society very often but represent merely a fuller and clearer apprehension of ideas which consciously or unconsciously permeate the thoughts and feelings of the entire race? In any case the ideas did reach the upper ten. Is it not surprising than that of the many millions of learned men who must have existed in the past in India not one should have left on record a protest, if the ideas of these Brahminical writers were so far divorced from facts? There is a remarkable protest against the so-called Brahminism—that from the prince of Epicureans, Charvaka—but even that protest shows that "Brahmanism" in fact permeated society and that this free-thinker was something like crying in the wilderness. And then, when was this great conspiracy of Brahmins started? When was their marvellous organisation—which permitted of no desertion and held India in a diamond net—when was it started and how was it maintained for thousands of years?

The story of the sudden influx of Brahminism upon the pure faith and habits of the people is a myth. The spirituality of their doctrine and the forms of ritual may have gained in depth and elaborateness with the progress of time but both the religious tone and the ritualism as well as the germs of their growth were already there in the earliest stage of society of which we can get a glimpse. If any confirmation were needed of this we could find it in a comparison of the Hindu shastras with the Vendidad of the Persians which would show a remarkable likeness in some of the fundamental spiritual and ritualistic ideas underlying the laws the two sets of scriptures (*r*). That would show that these ideas are traceable at least to the days before the Hindus and Persians separated. Indeed we may go further and say that a religious foundation for law as a whole as well as of every legal rule is the ruling idea of all primitive law.

To hold that secular custom proceeded along a course of development to a certain stage and then a sudden onset of ponti-

(*r*) Zend Avesta. Darmesteters translation Part I pp. 11 et seq. The likeness is more noticeable in the fundamental ideas than in details. The Chapter on impurities however teems with agreements in detail with Hindu ideas.

fical influence transformed these simple facts into elaborate rituals or religious institutions would be to repeat the historical error of the theorists who proclaimed the authority of a law of Nature. If comparative law has established any fact more clearly than any other, it is that the simple and essential fact in a juridical relation is first conceived under a more or less elaborate form and it is only in the course of its evolution that the essential fact is separated from the form. It is a gratuitous assumption to suppose that Indian legal history was an exception to that rule. A more proper view would be to hold that the religious and ceremonial form or theory under which simple jural relations are conceived in the Smritis were the forms in which they first obtained recognition. In course of time they have obtained, in a simpler form, in certain countries and amongst certain classes, but the simpler form was not the original one. Thus for instance the institution of adoption which is now conceived as a purely secular institution, for instance, in the Punjab, may very well have been first conceived under the spiritualistic idea with which we find it clothed in Smritis. That it was accompanied by the formalities required for it by Vasistha (1) seems to be certain. Spiritual relation between father and son which the Smritis conceive to be its essence must have existed prior to the recognition of the validity of adoptions. For kinship could not, unless it was conceived as essentially spiritual, be transferred by fiction to the adopted child. It may be that, with the progress of time some people might have preferred to look at the affair as what it really was, a device to leave one's property to a child of ones choice, neglecting the spiritual ideas under which the relationship was first conceived. But that was undoubtedly a later development and not a primary fact in the history of the law.

There is no reason to suppose therefore that the spiritual and ritualistic element in the law as we find it in the Smriti literature was an exotic growth, out of touch with the realities of the jural relations of ancient India. On the other hand all indications show that these formed essential parts of jural relations of those times. There is nothing therefore to discredit the claims of the legal philosophy of the Hindus to represent opinions that were actually held and applied in practice.

It is true that the Smritis were not mere records of customs as they actually obtained but of these as partially idealised and

---

(1) पुत्रं प्रतिग्रहिष्यन् बन्धूनाहूय राजनि चावेद्य निवेशनस्य मध्ये व्याहृतिभिर्हुत्वा बान्धवसन्निकृष्टमेव। Vasistha XV, 6.

viewed with reference to some special theories. But so were the works of Roman jurists ; and the theories of the Smritis were ,like those of Roman jurisconsults, merely formulas for the expression of a number of juridical facts under a general rule. The function which these theories exercised in the further development of law was likewise similar to that of the theories of the jurisconsults. Theories which were evolved to explain one set of facts would naturally lead by logical deduction to new rules and perhaps to new jural facts. Being general propositions embracing a number of isolated facts, these theories would rapidly pass out of the sphere of speculation and themselves become a part and parcel of the actual law and the source of new rules of law. Thus though the Smritis are no doubt to a certain extent founded on theory, the theories they embody have since ages become a part and parcel of the actual laws of the people.

PART II.

THE SOURCES OF LAW.

§1 GENERAL.

The sources of law which are recognised and referred to by the commentaries are numerous. Of these Sruti, Smriti and Achara are of primary importance. But besides these, personal preference, Reason, Parishads, learned Brahmans, the Puranas, Mimansa, Vedangas, Itihasas and the other vidyâs are all referred to for authority. In Yajnavalkya and Manu amongst the Smritis we find the most exhaustive enumerations of the sources of law. Yajnavalkya (*t*) gives the following:

(1) Sruti, (2) Smriti, (3) Good custom, (4) Whatever is agreeable to one's self, (5) Desire born of deliberation, (6) Parishad, (7) One well versed in Brahmavidyâ, (8) Puranas, (9) Nyaya, (10) Dharmasastras, (11) Angas, (12) Societies, such as village or caste community etc., (13) The King, (14) Custom, irrespective of whether they fall under the description of sadâchara or not (in conquered countries).

Manu's enumeration of the sources of law is equally comprehensive. Here also Sruti, Smriti and Custom enjoy a primary position while the rest are referred to incidentally (*u*).

Going back from these to Gautama, Apastamba, Baudhâyana and Vasistha we are struck with the meagreness of the enumera-

---

(*t*) श्रुतिः स्मृतिः सदाचारः स्वस्य च प्रियमात्मनः ।
सम्यक् संकल्पजः कामो धर्म्ममूलमिदं स्मृतम् ॥ I, 7.
चत्वारो वेदधर्म्मज्ञाः पर्षत् त्रैविद्यमेव वा ।
यं सा ब्रुते स धर्म्मः स्यादेकोऽपि ब्रह्मवित्तमः । I, 9.
पुराणन्यायमीमांसा धर्म्मशास्त्राङ्ग मिश्रिताः ।
वेदाः स्थानानि विद्यानां धर्म्मस्य तु चतुर्द्दश ॥ I, 3.
निजधर्म्माविरोधेन यत्तु सामयिको भवेत् ।
सोऽपि यत्नेन संरक्ष्यो धर्म्मो राजकृतश्च यत् ॥ II, 186.
श्रेणी नैगम पाषण्डि गणानामप्ययं विधिः ।
भेदञ्चैषां नृपो रक्षेत् पूर्व्ववृत्तिञ्च पालयेत् ॥ II, 192.
यस्मिन्देशे य आचारः व्यवहारः कुलस्थितिः ।
तथैव प्रतिपाल्योऽसौ यदा वशमुपागतः ॥ I, 343.

(*u*) Manu I, 118 II 6—18. VIII, 3, 41.

tion with which they start. Gautama refers to :—(1) Veda as the primary source and (2) the usages and recollections of those who known the law as the sources of dharma (*v*). But elsewhere he enumerates other sources as evidencing the law viz., (3) Dharmasastras, (4) Angas, (5) Upavedas, (6) Purana, (7) Customs of countries, races and Kulas in so far as these are not opposed to the Srutis (*w*), (8) Communities of herdsmen, traders and money-lenders in respect of affairs touching them (*x*), (9) learned Brahmans (*y*), (10) Parishads (*z*). In the enumeration of the qualifications of learned Brahmans he brings in the other vidyas and practices (*a*).

Apastamba gives the Veda and the agreement of learned men as the sources of law (*b*). He refers however to custom approved by Aryas (*c*) as having force in so far as they raised a presumption of their being founded on Sruti (*d*). He further refers to Parishads (*e*) and the usual Vidyâs, to the custom of countries and tribes (*f*) and to what Haradatta understands to mean Arthasastra (*g*).

Vasistha and Baudhâyana agree in referring to Veda, Smriti and Sishtâchâra as sources of law (*h*). Baudhàyana also refers to

---

(*v*) Gautama I, 1—2 वेदो धर्म्ममूलं तद्विदाञ्च स्मृतिशीले ।

(*w*) वेदो धर्म्मशास्त्राणि अङ्गानि उपवेदाः पुराणं देशजातिकुलधर्म्माश्च आम्नायैरविरुद्धः । XI, 19, 20.

(*x*) कृषिवणिक पाशुपाल्य: कुसीदकारव: स्वे स्वे वर्गे । XI, 21.

(*y*) XI, 25 ; XXVIII, 50.

(*z*) XXVIII 48, 49.

(*a*) VIII, 4—11, बहुश्रुत: is defined as लोकवेदवेदाङ्ग विद्वाक्येतिहास पुराण कुशलस्तद्वपेक्षस्तद्वृत्तिश्चत्वारिंशता संस्कारै संस्कृत: त्रिषु कर्म्मस्वभिरत: षट्सु वा सामयाचारिकेष्वभिविनीत: ।

(*b*) धर्म्मज्ञसमय: प्रमाणम् वेदाश्च । Apastamba I, 1, 2—3.

(*c*) यत्त्वार्य्या: क्रियमाणं प्रशंसन्ति स धर्म्मो यद्गर्हन्ते सोऽधर्म्म: । I, 1, 20, 7—8 See also II, 29, 14.

(*d*) He refers to âchara as आनुमानिक in I, 4, 8.

(*e*) अभ्युदत: परिषत्सु, I, 11, 38.

(*f*) II, 15, 1.

(*g*) II, 29, 15.

(*h*) उपदिष्टो धर्म्म: प्रतिवेदम् । * * स्मार्त्तो द्वितीय: । तृतीय: शिष्टागम: । Baudhayana I, 1, 1, 2—4. वेदस्मृति विहितोधर्म्म:, तदलाभे शिष्टाचार: प्रमाणम् । Vasistha I, 4—5.

Angas and Mimansa as relevant to the study of law (*i*) Parishads (*j*) are referred to by both as well as the customs of countries, castes and families (*k*).

From these enumerations we find that Sruti is the source of law *par excellence* and might be referred to as in one sense the formal source of law, Smriti stands next in order. Custom follows next. The Parishads, Puranas, Mimansa, etc., come after them.

If we look at these enumerations in the light of the of the observations relating to the state of society in ancient India in the foregoing pages it would appear that the Smritis represent the triumph of the religious principle and of the religious-military society over every other. If we look back to a stage indicated by the Smritis themselves but prior to the times therein depicted, we can conceive the community as consisting of a number of societies imperfectly co-ordinated with one another, each of which controlled the lives of the members of that particular society. Each of these societies had bodies of rules equally definite or indefinite and enforced by equally definite sanctions. Each had likewise its own source of law, in the sense of an authority which had power to lay it down. With the integration of the commonwealth into the semi-theocratic state these societies were gradually thrown into a heirarchy under the authority of religion and state and the sources of law naturally tended to fall into a system founded upon an assumption of the supreme authority of the religious law. Thus, the organ of authority in the religious society was the Parishad and in a minor degree every learned Brahman ; that in the military society was the king or chief ; while trade was ruled by its own guilds ; communities like those of Chandâlas, had their own assemblies ; and villages regulated their own affairs. All these authorities were recognised in the Smritis but only within limited spheres of their own and all the rest subject to the supreme authority of the religious law.

The religious law was at one time studied and proclaimed by the Parishads. In laying it down they habitually went by the traditions that prevailed in them and by approved usages. These were naturally looked upon as sacred. The sanctity of these traditions and approved usages had already been affiliated in the tradition of the Parishads with the Sruti which had begun to stand

---

(*i*) I, 1, 8.
(*j*) I, 1, 8, **Vasistha III, 7.**
(*k*) **Vasistha I, 17, XIX, 7.**

for the sum total of knowledge. When thus the law came to be enunciated in the Dharmasastras which were manuals embodying the traditions in the Parishads, Sruti or Veda was referred to as the primary source of all law. The Angas were aids to the study and interpretation of the knowledge that was, or was supposed to be, contained in the Vedas and these with the other Vidyas habitually studied in the Parishads thus gained access in the legal literature if not as sources, at any rate as important aids, to the proper understanding of laws.

The sources of law recognised by the Smritis therefore fall under two classes—those associated with religion and those appertaining to the various other societies. The latter had a sort of permissive status while the former enjoyed pre-eminence, subject to the authority of the Veda. In the following discussion I shall deal first with the sources of religious law and next with the secular customs and ordinances.

§2. Sruti as Source of Law.

When we hear Sruti or Veda spoken of as a source of law we have to remember what precisely the words 'Law' and 'Veda' stand for. Veda embraces the whole body of Vedic literature including the four Samhitas together with the Brâhmanas Aranyakas and Upanishads. So far as Veda is referred to as a source of law in the older works it is only the Brahmanas and Aranyakas that are primarily meant. For the Samhitas are very poor in precepts (*vidhi*). In the Brâhmanas and Aranyakas on the other hand such precepts abound.

By law (*dharma*) these authors did not understand merely that portion of normative rules which we should now call legal but all rules seeking to mould the religious, social and, to a very great extent, the personal life of man. It includes not only laws proper, not even the whole body of *Sâmayâcharika* rules dealt with in the Dharmasutras alone but also rules of ritual dealt with in the Srauta and Grihya codes. Law proper in fact was conceived by them as part of a comprehensive scheme of life ; and, when the Veda is referred to as authority for law, the latter term is understood as indicating rules embracing this life as a whole. Now, in this sense the Sruti is undoubtedly a source of practical rules, for the Srauta and Grihya sutras are based, to no small extent, on the texts of Brahmanas to which references are often made.

When however the Vedas are referred to as authority for Sâmayachârika rules in the Smritis, more is meant by the term than the particular texts of the Veda. For the Vedas cannot be looked upon as concrete sources of legal rules in the same sense that they are sources of many Srauta and Grihya rules. Apastamba himself practically admits that these rules cannot be found in the Vedas themselves, only he puts it in an orthodox fashion when he says that it is difficult to learn the law from the Vedas themselves and that therefore we must have recourse to custom approved by the Aryas to ascertain the law (*l*).

I take it therefore that at the time when Vedas were referred to in the Dharmasutras, the word had acquired an extended significance. It did not stand merely for concrete Vedic texts but rather represented a theory and texts of the Vedas themselves were viewed as representing something more than themselves.

Already in the Srauta and the Grihya sutras we find a theory about the *Sruti* developed. Though many of the rules of these works could be traced to the Brahmanas, not all that there is in them could be so traced. All rules however are alike referred to the ultimate authority of the Veda. This authority is entirely hypothetical ; those who appeal to it do not themselves know where in the concrete Vedic texts it is to be found. They suppose them sometimes to be referible to lost srutis and at others to be traceable in some of the innumerable sâkhas of the Vedas only a small fraction of which may be known to any man or perhaps even to a god. That is really a confession that the reference to the Srauta authority for these rules was entirely hypothetical. The fact is that these rules are founded on tradition and approved pratices and the theory is that they must be found in the Veda. That may also be said of almost the whole of the rules of the Dharmasutras.

It would seem then that 'Veda' had ceased to signify merely the aggregate of sacred revealed texts known to the writers but stood for the sum total of actual and possible knowledge and the embodiment of all moral and religious truths. There could be no truth but was in the Veda, no law but is originally laid down, may be, by a mere slight indication, in the Veda ; there is no approved practice which is not founded on the Veda. It is the embodiment of eternal knowledge and eternal law, older than the world and co-eval with the Supreme Being himself. It was revealed to the elect amongst men ; but of the eternal code thus revealed to mankind all over the world only a fraction could be known to any man. Much of what was revealed had moreover

(*l*) Apastamba II, 29, 13.

been lost. But Vedic rules thus lost or beyond our ken could be known by following approved practices and the traditions handed down from the seers themselves.

This theory was at its inception the result of the integration of two ideas which we find characterising the thoughts of men in all primitive societies. One was the notion that whatever knowledge was not syllogistically worked out but came rather by flashes of intuition, must be inspired knowledge. The other idea is that customs which have come down from ancestors must be sacred. Custom is habit become self-conscious, but, with its emergence into self-consciousness, habit gathers round itself a halo of sanctity ;—people follow it with awe as something supernaturally ordained. To a people given to contemplation, as the Indo-Aryans undoubtedly were, it was but natural that the sanctity of knowledge and that of custom should be welded together into one and both referred to a common source. So we find that so soon as attempts are made to understand the character of this knowledge and custom with more precision than is implied in the vague consciousness of their sanctity, they are both regarded as founded on the Eternal Word which is alike the spring of truth and of virtue. The extant sacred works, as well as any piece of inspired knowledge that was newly acquired, would be naturally regarded as parts of that eternal code ; but not even the whole body of known texts could be looked upon as exhausting the contents of the Veda.

It is this hypothetical Veda rather than the extant Vedic texts that the authors of the Dharmasutras had in mind when they referred to Veda as the original source of all law. It was more or less of a symbol for expressing their reverence to sacred customs and traditions and very little more. It is remarkable that in the works of Gautama, Apastamba Vasistha, Baudhâyana and Vishnu there is scarcely any attempt to trace back any particular rules which they lay down to extant Sruti texts such as we find in the commentators and notably in Kumarilaswâmi. This they did not deem to be really necessary, and, once they had made their homage to the Veda by recognising it as the source of law, they were content to give the exposition of the law itself as they found it embodied in sacred tradition and approved usage. Apastamba quite frankly says almost as much (*m*).

Of course the extant Vedic texts were recognised as authoritative and, when one came by the way, its authority had to be

---

(*m*) Apastamba loc cit, also I, 1, 1.

acknowledged. If none was at hand the authority of the Veda would, all the same, go unquestioned on the hypothesis that it must be founded on some Sruti either lost or not known to the author. Such revealed texts must be inferred as the foundations of the traditional rules (*n*).

But the recognition of the authority of the Vedas could not for ever stop here. As the Vedas and Dharmasastras were more and more read there would be a tendency to confront a rule of the latter with one to be found in the former. We already find a tendency towards that in the works of Apastamba, Vasistha and Baudhayana and also in a smaller degree in Gautama. Perhaps such a tendency has to be referred back further still, as without such enquiries and the problems that they might suggest there would be no occasion for the development of some of the Mimansa rules of interpretation which these authors refer to. But it was in far later times that the tendency grew really formidable. The result of the growth of this tendency which we find in its germ in the Dharmasastras was the elaboration of a number of exegetic rules some of which are referred to as matters of course by these authors (*o*).

The attempt to reconcile the provisions of the Dharmasastras with the Sruti would involve the question as to how far the Sruti is authoritative. Now, it goes without question with all, that when you get a genuine text of the Veda laying down a rule of law, that has paramount power and, according to the generally accepted opinion, power to override a contrary text of the Dharmasastras. But are all texts of the Vedas to have that authority? On this question scholars were divided. Vedic texts are classified under three main heads, *Vidhis* or injunctions, Arthavâdas or mere recital and *Mantras* or words to be uttered at religious functions (*p*). One school would say that neither *arthavâdas* nor *Mantras* are at all authoritative, it is only vidhis, which are in the form of commands, that are to be regarded as authoritative. If Apastamba does not go so far as that, he surely refuses to recognise a mere narration of a fact as laying down an authoritative rule. So where the Veda says "Manu divided his wealth among his sons", it is to be taken, according to Apastamba, as a state-

(*n*) See for instance Apastamba I, 12, 10. For the nature of the authority of such customs see post. Part II §4.

(*o*) Apastamba makes several references to Mimansa rules e.g. 1, 12, 10—11 ; Gautama too in I, 3—4 is also hinting at some such rules. See *post* Part II §7—*Mîmânsa.*

(*p*) *Tantravârttika*, Benares edition p. 1.

ment of a fact which does not embody an authoritative rule of law (*q*) Jaimini on the other hand, as interpreted by Sabaraswami and Kumarilaswami gives a contrary decision and looks upon every text of the Sruti as authoritative. The scope of authority of each class of rules may be limited by the nature of the rule, but in every case a text has some authority (*r*).

The Mimansa view seems to represent a later stage in the development of the Sruti theory. In any case, it made it possible to refer to a number of Vedic texts as authorities for legal rules which could not otherwise be recognised as having any legal bearing. Thus for instance on the question as to whether a father has the right of property over his children, the controversialists might refer to the texts of the Katha Upanishad where Nâchiketa is given to Yama by his father who was performing a Viswajit sacrifice (*s*). In the later controversies where rules of the Smritis are confronted with Vedic rules we find references to many such texts which Apastamba would have explained away as bare statements of fact.

I have said before that, historically, tradition and usage must have been the primary sources, the foundation of law upon which the superstructure of the Sruti theory was raised. In the older Dharmasastras, in spite of their recognition of the superior claims of Sruti, we yet find indications of a stage when tradition and usage enjoyed practical primacy in matter of *Achâra*. Gautama no doubt refers for the sources of law to the Vedas and the practices and tradition handed down from the seers in the same breath (*t*). But Apastamba who in many respects represents an earlier stratum of thought refers to the agreement of learned men as the primary practical source of law and refers to the Veda only as the ultimate source of the authority of rules so laid down (*u*). This would seem to indicate a stage of thought when, subject to the theoretic recognition of the Vedic authority, the decisions of

(*q*) Apastamba II, 14, 13.

(*r*) An arthavâda has in this view to be read as a part of a Vidhi, read along with which alone it ceases to be redundant (अनर्थक) See on this Jaimini I ii Adh I, with Sabara's commentary and Kumarila's *Tantra-varttika* (Benares ed.) p. 1 et seq.

(*s*) Katha Upanishad Chap I ; This story is referred to in Vyavahara Mayukha in its discussion on that subject.

(*t*) Gautama I, 1.

(*u*) धर्म्मज्ञसमय: प्रमाणम्, वेदाश्च । Apastamba I, 2—3 ; which Haradatta rightly interprets as implying that the Vedas are the ultimate foundation of the *samaya*.

parishads and the traditions of the sages carried practically the primary authority. But the recognition of the authority of the Vedas was bound in the long run to affect the authority of these primary sources and as texts of the Vedas were confronted with rules of other origin, these had to give way to the former. So that from their primary position these rules sank to the position of secondary sources of law, raising merely a presumption of their srauta origin ; and, with the progress of time, more and more stringent tests were laid down for custom and tradition, tests which they must satisfy in order to raise a presumption of Vedic origin.

What the exact relation between Sruti and Smriti or Custom was we shall be in a better pesition to consider when we have discussed the position of these latter as sources of law.' I may however briefly summarise here the conclusions which I draw with reference to the Sruti. To start with, we find the Sruti as a mere theory—a formula for expressing the sanctity of custom and traditional knowledge by a single conception. The theory, however, when it said that the Sruti was the source of all law, would not be in conformity with facts. Such conformity was established however by the two-fold process of approximation by which a theory is made to correspond with facts.

In the first place, the Sruti theory was expanded, on the one hand, by the rules of interpretation which made it possible to find rules of law in texts which would otherwise yield none, and on the other, by a hypothesis of lost sakhas on which Smritis and Customs were founded. The practical sources of law on their part approximated to the Sruti by ceasing to be the primary sources and claiming authority by raising a mere presumption of srauta authority. The main instrument in producing the final conformity between Sruti and Smriti was interpretation, by which, on the one hand, sruti was made to yield rules of law and, on the other, all the practical sources of law were harmonised into a system under the supreme authority of the Sruti. When from being a mere theory, Sruti was developed into a practical source of law, it had an important reaction on the further development of law, most notably, by restricting the scope of custom as a source of law, and, generally speaking, by giving a scholastic character to the later expositions of the law in the commentaries. These abound in dialectical subtleties necessitated by the need for harmonising or explaining away a text of Sruti which was looked upon as having a bearing on the law.

But with all these developments the scope of the sruti in its application to strictly juridical rules was very small indeed. It exercised a more pronounced influence on the other aspects of Achara.

§ Smriti and Parishads.

The word Smriti literally means Recollection, or what is remembered. The word as used in text books on Hindu law has however the meaning which Manu assign to it, viz., the Dharma-sâstras (*v*). These are regarded as sources of law and meant by the expression Smriti by Manu and Yâjnavalkya (*w*). Smriti as a source of law is also mentioned by the older authors. Gautama, for instance refers to the *sila* (practices) and *Smriti* (Recollection) of those who know the Vedas as sources of law (*x*). Vasistha refers to Veda and Smriti as sources of law (*y*). Baudhâyana also refers to Smriti as a secondary source of law (*z*). Apastamba on the other hand refers, not to the recollections, but to the "agreements" of learned men (*a*) though perhaps meaning the same thing.

The sense in which this word has been used by these authors appears to be different from that implied by authors like Manu and Yâjnavalkya. In the latter set of authors 'Smriti' has a technical (योगरूढ़) meaning, it means the Dharmasastras and nothing more ; and those authors as well as Parâsara and others take care to enumerate the authoritative Smritis (*b*). Gautama however evidently uses the term in a clearly non-technical sense. He qualifies the word *smriti* by adding "of those who know the Veda" (*c*). Vasistha is more doubtful, but having reference to the form of his expression I am disposed to take him as referring to Smriti in its non-technical sense (*d*). Baudhayana however shows a distinct learning towards the technical sense (*e*). In Manu too we find the older tradition represented by one of the

---

(*v*) श्रुतिस्तु वेदो विज्ञेयो धर्मशास्त्रं तु वै स्मृतिः । Manu II, 10.

(*w*) Manu II, 6, 10, 12. Yâjn. I, 7.

(*x*) Gautama I, 1.

(*y*) Vasistha I, 4.

(*z*) Baudhâyana I, 1, 3 ;

(*a*) Apâstamba I, 1, 2.

(*b*) Yajnavalkya I, 4—5 Parasara I, 13—15. The number however tends to increase and in the Garuda Purana we have 18 Smritis. Paithinasi gives 25 and Hemâdri 55 Smritis and Mitra Misra 57.

(*c*) Gautama I, 2.

(*d*) Vasistha I, 4.

(*e*) Baudhâyana I, 1, 3.

texts where he uses the term not alone but as the "Smriti of those who know the Veda" (*f*).

I have suggested before that Apastamba in referring to the "agreement' of those who know the Dharma" was not really referring to a different source of law. Gautama and Apastamba meant the same thing. It will be seen that Gautama does not require anything more for the Smriti than that it should be that of men who know the Veda and *a fortiori* the sacred law. When Apastamba is referring to the *Samaya* of such men he does not mean that they are mere arbitrary resolutions of learned men but rather assumes that these men proceed to determine the law according to their knowledge and recollection of the sacred law.

We shall pause for one moment to consider the full import of Apastamba's text. Apastamba calls the rules of law laid down in his Dharmasastras *Sâmayâchârika* rules (*g*). Nor was he singular in the use of the word, for we find Gautama also using the same expression (*h*). *Sâmayâcharika,* according to Haradatta, means "consisting of customs settled by human agreement" (*i*). If, as we find from Gautama, the word was an old one we find further confirmation of the view that Apastamba in refering to "agreement" as source of law was following an old tradition.

That law is founded on some sort of agreement, though it is ultimately of divine origin, is an idea which we find cropping up among all Aryan races at the earlier stages of the development of their law. Thus in Rome so late a jurist as Papinian says, among other definitions of law that it is "a resolution on the part of learned men" (*j*). Hermogenianus finds the foundation of authority of long established custom in "a tacit agreement on the part of citizens in general" (*k*). Marcianus quotes Demosthenes as defining law as "something which all men ought to obey chiefly because every law is devised and given by God, but resolved on by intelligent men * * * a general agreement by the community by which all men living therein ought to order their lives" (*l*). It is a sign of the persistence of the conception in

(*f*) Mann II 6 वेदोऽखिलं धर्ममूलं स्मृतिशीले च तद्विदाम्।

(*g*) Apastamba I, 1, 1.

(*h*) Gautama VIII 11.

(*i*) पौरुषेयी व्यवस्था समयः, समयमूलाः आचाराः समयाचाराः, एवम्भूतान् धर्मान्।

(*j*) Justinian, Digest Book I Tit. iii, 1.

(k) *Ibid.* I, iii, 35.

(*l*) Digest I, iii, 2.

Aryan thought that the idea of law being founded on some sort of agreement recurs in the writings of modern jurists like Locke, Hobbes and Rousseau no less than in Savigny and Puchta. Korkunov looks upon these theories about the foundation of law on an ultimate agreement as based on a fiction (*n*). Whether that is so if we look back to the earliest glimpses of law to which sociological researches introduce us we need not here consider. But the tenacity with which the idea of agreement clings to the Aryan mind is a fact that seems to point to a different conclusion so far as historical law is concerned.

There can be little doubt that, in early Aryan societies, law was invariably looked upon as founded on the twin roots of religion and agreement of men learned in sacred lore. Societies with such ideas would naturally be expected to look to assemblies of wise men to lay down the law and such assemblies are to be found in every primitive Aryan society of which we can trace the history back far enough. One might almost say that the vesting of the authority in these assembles is a trait that most remarkably distinguishes the polity, history and mythology of Aryans as a body from those of, say, the Semites with their autocratic Judges, Prophets and Kings. The Pontiffs of Rome, the Druids of Bretain, the Witan of the Saxons and similar institutions all over the early Aryan world illustrate these early associations of men vested with knowledge of the sacred law.

It was on account of this origin of their laws that the theory of the foundation of law on agreement seems to have struck such a deep root in the minds of Aryan races.

The Indian Aryan too had such an institution in the dim past. It was the Parishad. In the Brihadaranyaka Upanishad we find that Svetaketu went for knowledge to the Parishad of the Pânchâlas (*n*). This meagre reference is not as barren of information as it appears at first sight to be, for we learn from it that a Parishad was an institution attached to a clan, that it was a centre of learning to which people fiocked for instruction, if we are to take Swetaketu's case as the general rule, upon the completion of the ordinary course of studies. It was here very likely that the ancient sages spent their life in contemplation and the pursuit of the knowledge of the Veda as well as of the sciences that clustered round the study of the Veda ; it was here that they elaborated the deep philosophical disquisitions which are em-

(*m*) Korkunov, General Theory of Law p. 411.

(*n*) श्वेतकेतुर्ह वा आरुणेयः पञ्चालानां परिषदमाजगाम, VI, 2.

bodied in the Upanishads. We can assume without any violence that these secluded sages exercised an all-round influence over the lives and actions of men in the community, upon their customs and their knowledge and the sciences (*o*).

Max Müller has hinted a connection between these Sâkhas and the Parishads and there is good reason to suppose that the Parishads had a great deal to do with the division of Vedic learning into the Sâkhas. *Prima facie* that conclusion would seem to be warranted by the name *prâtisâkhya* given to a class of what are called Pârshada works or works associated with a Parishad. What seems to have happened is that these various clan Parishads situated in different parts of the country each retained and pursued the study of one or the other or more than one of the Vedas. When the Vedas were retained by word of the mouth variations in the readings would naturally crop up and upon these would be based a division of the Vedas ino the various Sâkhas. The term came to imply both a recension of the Veda which was followed in any particular Parishad and the body of men who followed the particular recension.

Possibly the division of Vedic *Sâkhas* into *charanas* which was undoubtedly a much later classification was also the result of a similar divergence in practices and codes of law obtaining in the various minor Parishads, which sprang out of the parent Parishad identified with the Sâkhas, after the texts of the Vedas themselves had become well settled in the various Sâkhas and possibly reduced to writing. The difference between one charana and another does not consist in any divergence in the Vedic texts in vogue in the charana but in the practices embodied in their respective Srauta, Grihya and Dharmasutras. These practices might continue to diversify, even after the Sâkhas had been settled, as sub-schools gathered round eminent scholars sent out by the parent Parishad who settled in distant parts of the country. The community of disciples of this scholar and those who habitually took their law from them would in time develop an individuality of its own by reason of their peculiar practices which would naturally be found, in course of time, to differ from those of the parent institution. The work which, at a later date, would embody the traditions and practices in this institution

(*o*) Max Müller (*History of Sanskrit Literature* p. 128) describes the Parishad as "an assembly which should be competent to give decisions on all points on which the people, or if we may say so, the parishioners might demand advice". "Such Parishads or Brahmanic settlements," he says, "existed in old times."

would differ in some respects at least from the work belonging to the parent school or other sub-schools growing out of it. The communities living under the authority of these institutions would be found to differ therefore in their rituals, practices and laws though retaining a common recension of the Veda. Such communities appear to have attracted to themselves at a later date the name of *Charanas*. The difference between them consisted mainly in the different works to which they looked for an authoritative declaration of laws and rituals.

The growth of what I should call the charana Parishads would mean the break up of the old clan Parishads, the constitutional assemblies with authority dictate law and sciences to the people of the clan. The movement would be hastened still further by the reduction of the laws of the charanas to writing. If you had written manuals giving authoritatively the traditions of the Parishad there would be little occasion to appeal to the Parishad for authority. Any learned scholar who had such a work with him would be quite as competent to give the necessary advice, at any rate, any company of learned men would be so. When people had such men at hand all over the country, the Parishads would naturally fall into decay. That appears to be what actually happened. For though the Smritis abound in texts which show the authority of the Parishads, they at the same time give an account of the nature of the Parishads which is very different from that of the Parishad of the Brihadâranyaka.

Gautama says that Parishad is an assemblage of ten men answering to a particular description (*p*) Vasistha (*q*) and Baudhâyana (*r*), while agreeing that the number should be ten, admits the possibility of a lesser number thus bringing the law into harmony with Yajnavalkya who sets down the number at four but seems to indicate that if the members of the *parshat* are versed in the three Vedas any number more or less would do. Yajnavalkya also places a single man of eminent spirituality in the

---

(*p*) चत्वारश्चतुर्णां पारगा: वेदानां प्रागुत्तमास्त्रय आश्रमिण: पृथग्धर्मविदस्त्रय: दशावरान् परिषदित्याचक्षते । XXVIII, 49.

(*q*) चातुर्विद्यो विकल्पी च अङ्गविद्धर्म पाठक: ।
आश्रमस्थास्त्रयीमुख्या: परिषत्स्यात् दशावर: ।
III, 20. (This is also given by Parasara VIII, 34.)
But in III 7, he mentions an assembly of four or three.

(*r*) Baudhâyana to the same effect I, 1, 7—9.

same position of authority as a Parishad (*s*) Parâsara also agrees in this reduction of the number of the Parishad (*t*).

While these references to the authority of the Parishad clearly indicate its old traditional authority, they make it clear that in the times when these works were composed the old tribal *parishad* of the Upanishads had been replaced by a body which was nothing more than the chance association of a number of learned men. The authority which the older Parishads enjoyed by tradition was thus transferred to any chance association of *savants*. The historical foundation of that authority was lost in obscurity and Yajnavalkya has no hesitation in placing the authority of the Parishad on the same footing as that of an eminently spiritual man. In the other Smritis also we find that single learned Brahman was authorised to lay down the law (*u*) and as such authority was given to him by the Dharmasastras, presumably a man who acted upon such advice, though it might be erroneous, would not be in the wrong.

If it was competent to a single Brahman scholar to lay down the law, a Parishad even in the attenuated form in which we find it in Yâjnavalkya would seem to be redundant. It seems to have appeared to the Smriti writes that such an objection might be made and it was possibly to explain this difficulty that Baudhâyana lays down that no one however learned should venture to lay down the law ; for, if his view of the law is wrong, he would incur sin and not the man who followed his advice (*v*). In a

---

(*s*) चत्वारो वेदधर्म्मज्ञाः पर्षत्त्रैविद्यमेव वा ।
यं सा ब्रूते स धर्म्मः स्यादेकोऽपि ब्रह्मवित्तम ॥ I, 9.

(*t*) चत्वारो वा त्रयोवाऽपि वेदवन्तोऽग्निहोत्रिणः ।
ब्राह्मणानां समर्था ये परिषत् सा विधीयते ॥
अनाहिताग्नयो येऽन्ये वेदवेदाङ्ग पारगाः ।
पञ्चत्रयो वा धर्म्मज्ञा परिषत् सा प्रकीर्त्तिता ॥
मुनीनामात्मविद्यानां द्विजानां यज्ञयाजिनां ।
वेदव्रतेषुस्नातानामेकोऽपि परिषद्भवेत् ॥
पञ्चपूर्व्वं मया प्रोक्तास्तेषां वाऽसम्भवे त्रयः ।
स्ववृत्तिपरितुष्टा ये परिषत् सा प्रकीर्त्तिता ॥

So Brihaspati cited by Madhava :

लोकवेदाङ्गधर्म्मज्ञाःसप्तपञ्च त्रयोवापि ।
यत्रोपविष्टाः विप्रा स्युः सा यज्ञसदृशी सभा ॥

(*u*) Gautama XXVIII 50. Baudhayana I, 1, 13 ; Vasistha I, 40.

(*v*) Baudhâyana I, i, 12.

Parishad where several men give an united opinion the sin is eliminated and no Prayaschitta is necessary for a wrong advice given by a Parishad. That is the new justification which has been put forward for the Parishad if not by the Smritis themselves, at any rate, by their interpreters.

The old Vedic Parishad was dead long ago, the Parishad of the Smritis too has long ceased to exist, at any rate, in its proper name. Even at the time when Haradatta wrote its memory appears to have been lost, for when Apastamba refers for other rules to the Parishads (*w*) Haradatta attempts to interpret 'Parishads' as implying the works of Manu and others. The Parishad however left its successors in the Universities and centres of learning of later days, to which people flocked for advice on all religious and legal matters and, perhaps, in the Kings' sabhâ which had in it all the elements of the Parishad of the Smritis and possibly helped in the extinction of the older Parishads by substituting for it a better organised institution which would naturally carry more authority in the actual decision of disputes.

I have referred above to Haradatta's peculiar interpretation of the term Parishad. It might be that Haradatta was not singular in his interpretation but that he was really following a tradition which prevailed in his day which called the Smritis Parishads or Pârshada works. There is at any rate this element of truth in his statement that the older Dharmasutras were merely embodiments of the traditional laws of particular Parishads. They were called along with the Srauta and Grihya Sutras, as well as the Prâtisâkyas and other works, Parishada works. That they were associated with the various charana Parishads appear to be clear, for the authors of the Dharmasastras are also founders of the various charanas (*x*). The ancient Dharmasastras are singularly devoid of any pretensions to superhuman authority such as is claimed for themselves by Manu, Yâjnavalkya and Narada. The sole foundation for their authority lies, with them, in their being records of sacred customs and traditions as they obtained in the Parishads. This remark can be made of the whole body of Dharmasutras extant, not excepting Vishnu,—for the portions in this last work which do claim a supernatural authority for itself are entirely out of touch with the main work and are clearly later additions. Apastamba makes his position perfectly clear. He claimed no supernatural authority but only to lay down rules

(*w*) Apastamba I, 11, 38.

(*x*) See Bühler Sacred Laws of the Aryas S. B. E. Introd p. xvi *et seq.*

which have been settled by the agreement of learned men. Then again, he disclaims on behalf of himself as well as of the *avaras* (latter day men) generally any pretensions to revealed knowledge. He says that the Rishis or seers of the Vedas had long ceased to exist but there had been amongst latter day men some srutarshis like Svetaketu who had attained supreme knowledge by reason of a residue of merit in a past life (*y*). That would indicate that he did not claim for himself even the status of a Srutarshi. Gautama too did not evidently claim to do anything more than lay down the sacred law as ascertained by tradition and custom (*z*). Nor did Baudhayana or Vasistha do so (*a*). The works of these authors are however referred to by later authors as included under Smritis in the technical sense, in the sense, that is, of works written by seers themselves recording the sacred law, derived, presumably, from their Vedic knowledge.

It is clear that these authors do not arrogate to themselves the position or seers or sages whose recollection would pass as authoritative. So they themselves would seem not to have included their own works under the source of law which they call Smriti. Nor could they possibly contemplate such a position for their works ; for, by Smriti which they referred to as a source of law they meant simply recollection and nothing more. The law they proposed is, no doubt, founded on Sruti, Smriti and approved custom but their work is as little to be identified with any of these sources as Blackstone's work is to be identified with any of the sources to which he refers the authority of law.

In course of time however these unauthoritative expositions of the law, partly by reason of their accurate representation of facts, partly on account of the eminence of their authors and the habitual obedience of people to the Parishads which they led and partly, perhaps, on account of their definite and systematic form alone, became hand-books in constant use with their pupils and the large body of men that guided their lives by their advice. They thus naturally tended to replace all other sources of law

---

(*y*) तस्मादृषयोऽवरेषु न जायन्ते नियमातिक्रमात्, श्रुतर्षयस्तु भवन्ति केचित् कर्मफलशेषेण पुनःसम्भवे, यथा श्वेतकेतुः ॥ Apastamba I, 5, 4—6.

(*z*) This appears to be the effect of the first and last Sutras of Gautama taken together.

(*a*) Medhatithi unconsciously hits a historical truth when he says, ये स्मरन्ति तेषामाप्यमेव तत्र शब्दादि प्रमाणं नात्मीया स्मृतिः यथास्माकन्तु मन्वादिस्मृतिरेव प्रमाणम् ।

for practical purposes and gradually, like the works of the Roman jurisconsults, came to be looked upon as immediate and authoritative sources of law. A later generation which already found these works enthroned in power had to furnish some justification for their authority and to bring it under some one or other of the recognised sources of law. These authors were canonised and their utterances were thus allowed to pass muster as Smriti or recollections or seer-sages. It was but a short step form this to the stage at which these works monopolised to themselves the name of Smriti and this word became a technical term signifying, as Manu says, what was known as Dharmasâstras. This new idea of Smriti we find fully well established in Manu and Yajnavalkya and elaborated in Jaimini's sutras and their commentaries.

I have attempted to trace above the history and the rise to authority of the Dharmasutras. The other class of works which pass by the name of Smriti—the metrical Dharmasâstras—were far different in character. Manu, Yâjnavalkya, Parâsara, Narada and a host of other metrical works, most of which do not deal with law at all, come forward with definite pretensions to authority. Of these Narada is admittedly an abridgement of Manu, though it may be doubted whether it was an abridged edition of the legal sections of Bhrigu's text. Parâsara is obviously a late compilation purporting to lay down the law for the later sinful days (Kaliyuga) for which all the other Dharmasastras which are enumerated would be unsuitable (*b*). The legal portion of Parâsara too is lost. Manu and Yâjnavalkya stand apart from all these other authors by reason of the great authority which their texts carry with all commentators and Nibandha writes.

Max Müller has given currency to an opinion which has received general acceptance that Manu's Code is a comparatively late compilation, that there was an original Manava Dharmasâstra which was written in sutra style and was the manual in use with the Manava charana of the Maitrâyaniya Sâkha (*c*).

(*b*) Parasara is however mentioned by Yajnavalkya as a Dharmasastra writer. That however may or may not mean that the present Parasarasamhita is anterior to Yajnavalkya. As I shall presently show, all these meterial Smritis were attempted reconstructions of lost works. There are many texts common to Parasara and Vasistha which are quoted by Baudhâyana without naming the author.

(*c*) History of Sanskrit Literature p. 133 et seq. Of metrical Smritis generally he says "There can be no doubt however that all genuine metrical Dharmasastras which we possess now are, without exception nothing but more modern texts of earlier Sutra works or *Kuladharma* (?) belonging originally to certain Vedic Charanas."

Any one who reads Manu critically would find it to be a compilation made up of texts which belong to widely different strata of thought. It cannot be doubted that in its present form it is a compilation founded, in no small degree, on old traditions. But one may yet keep an open mind about the hypothesis of Manu's code being founded on a lost Sutra work of the Manavas. The only authority for this theory is the fact of the existence of a Mânava charana vouched for by a comparatively late work, the Charanavyuha. Even assuming that that charana had a manual which passed by Manu's name it does not follow that that was the only form in which the Laws of Manu existed in the past. Manu may as well have also been the name of a comparatively late founder of a charana or a late charana may very well have sought to have traced a fictitious affinity to Manu as their eponymous spiritual ancestor. Instances of such attempts to add a fictitious importance to one's lineage or spiritual ancestry are not quite rare either in India or elsewhere. All these are possibilities which may well make us hesitate to accept without reserve Max Müller's theory of the descent of the Manu's Code from a Dharmasutra of the Mânava charana.

The division of Vedic learning into the various charanas is, as I have pointed out, a comparatively late event. For we do not find in Vedic literature or in the Smritis, any mention of the charanas though the Sâkhas represented important divisions in those days. But Manu as a lawgiver is known from the very earliest times. In Vedic tradition Manu is the first born of God who creates the rest of the beings and establishes order amongst them (*d*). The tradition varies in the Mahabharata, the Ramayana and Puranas but one thing is always insisted on in these works viz. that Manu was the ancestor of the human race and its first law-giver. Vedic texts vouch for the authority and sanctity or whatever Manu has said (*e*) and Kumarilaswami was surely right in taking these texts as implying an authority in a Manu to lay down binding rules. That, of course, does not show that this Manu did compile any code of laws. On the contrary the idea of compiling such a code would possibly belong to a much later stratum of thought. I refer to this to show only the antiquity of the Manu tradition upon which was founded the authority of the Code under his name, no matter when compiled. That a

---

(*d*) Kathaka Samhita XI, 5 and other places.

(*e*) यत्तु मनुरब्रवीत्तद्भेषज: text of the Taittiriya Samhita cited in Tantravarttika and Parasara Madavyam.

body of rules passed under the name of Manu at perhaps a later date than the Vedic times and attracted to itself all the authority that attached to the name of Manu in tradition is undoubted. Of the extant Dharmasutras all refer to him and Vasistha and Baudhâyana make copious quotations from his sayings (*f*). These authors refer to Manu, not as mere author of a Dharmasastra whose opinion is open to controversy but as an absolutely binding authority (*g*). It is clear therefore that in the days when these Dharmasutras were written Manu's authority as the first law-giver was unhesitatingly acknowledged and legal texts and maxims that passed under his name had been completely affiliated with the ancient Manu tradition.

As to the style of the sayings of the original Manu it is impossible to speak with assurance. Reference has been made to some quotations from Manu in the Sutras which were not in verse; from this it has been assumed that the original Manu was in prose or perhaps in mixed prose and verse like Gautama, Apastamba, Vishnu, Vasistha and Baudhâyana. But it is difficult to say that is conclusive. For it does not appear to be anything like clear that prose quotations from Manu were not mere paraphrases of the original. At any rate we find that the verse quotations are certainly very much more numerous then the prose extracts. Max Müller's dictum that the Sutra form of writing was anterior to the metrical is by no means countenanced by the fact that the sutra authors themselves quote gâthâs in verse as widely current (*h*)

(*f*) See Gautama XXI, 7 XXIII, 28 ; Vasistha I, 17 ; III, 2 ; XI, 23 ; XII, 16 ; XIII. 16 XIX, 37 ; XXIII 4, 3, Baudhayana II, 3, 2 ; IV 1, 13 ; 2, 15, 1. Vishnu and Manu have too many points of contact to demand mention. Parasara I, 13 and Yajnavalkya I, of course refer to Manu first among lawgiers. Brihaspati is quoted as saying :

मन्वर्थविपरीता या सा स्मृतिर्न प्रशस्यते ।

वेदार्थो हि निबन्धृत्वात् प्राधान्यो हि:मनोः स्मृतः ॥

(*g*) Other authors are referred to and supported or refuted in the Dharmasutras, notably in Gautama and Apastamba. Apastamba refers to and controverts Svetaketu, Kanva, Kautsa, Varshayani, Kunika, Pushkarasadi. A Prajapati of ten mentioned by Vasistha and Apastamba may possibly be the same as Daksha.

(*h*) Many of these are cited by Vasistha see for example I, 15. Most of the verses quoted by Apastamba, Gautama and others are such gâthâs or current sayings in verse. Gâthâs are mentioned by Yajnavalkya as subjects the study of which brings merit like that of the Puranas, catechisms, itihâsas and other studies (Yajn I, 45). The Mitakshara mentions "Yajnagatha, Indragatha, etc.," as illustrations of gâthâs apparently current in its time.

and I have not come across any cogent argument not drawn largely from imagination which establishes that the sutra works must needs precede any attempt to remember things by reducing them to verse. So that, we must conclude that a great many at least of the texts attributed to Manu in those ancient times were, and all of them might well have been, in verse.

So far then we do not get any authority for the existence of any sutra work attributed to Manu, upon the basis of which the metrical Manu was composed. Nor is there any evidence of it any where in literature except the very indirect one drawn from the existence of the name Mânava as that of a charana (*i*). Even assuming all that is claimed for that piece of evidence, where do we get it that all the charanas had written works of law, not to speak of those works being in sutra style? We have not got more than half-a dozen sets of sutras which are traceable to some of the charanas. That evidence leaves the general proposition based upon it a mere unproved hypothesis.

We get it, however, that there was abroad a number of texts attributed to Manu, mostly in verse, which were recognised as authoritative. Whether there was or was not a complete work containing these texts at any time must for the present remain a mere speculation. I am inclined to believed that such a complete work was not known to Vasistha or Baudhâyana for, if it was, their essays in the same line would naturally be deemed unfruitful and redundant, regard being had to the absolutely binding character of Manu's authority in their eyes. Their works appear to have been attempts to systematise a body of laws which were scattered about but not embodied in any definite *authoritative* treatise known to them. Be that as it may, the complete work if it ever existed must have been entirely lost in later times. Manu's wisdom was scattered about in a number of saying which passed from mouth to mouth.

I am disposed to look upon the extant Code of Manu not as a deliberate forgery on a wholesale scale, but, rather, as an honest attempt to reconstruct the lost Code of Manu from materials furnished by his current sayings. These were pieced together and systematised, additions were made to fill up the lacunae, to make the texts correspond to current practice, and, altogether, to make the work comprehensive and in every respect worthy

(*i*) The principal works belonging to the Mânava Charana have been found and they do not at all show remarkable agreements with Manusamhita. (See Jolly: *Tagore Law Lectures* p. 47). That would go to discredit the Mânava theory of the Manusamhita.

of the great teacher. That the compilation thus made contained very largely the texts popularly ascribed to Manu is certain. Otherwise it could not have risen to the authority it attained to by reason of its association with Manu's name. The fact that quotations from Manu in old sutra works can be verified in the extant Code also points to the same conclusion. As for the additions, it is possible that some of them may have grown as the sayings went from mouth to mouth. Others may have been deliberately constructed. It is quite clear moreover that the work was also developed by later hands than those of the compiler. This would be done by adding newly discovered texts attributed to Manu which were unknown to the original compiler, as well as by deliberate additions in the spirit in which Madhvâchâryya in historical times inserted a vyavahara section of his own composition in Parâsara's work.

Who did the compiling of the work and under what circumstances must be a matter of pure speculation. The tradition preserved in Manu's Code itself and vouched for by Narada may have in it some element of truth. The compilation was very possibly done by a Bhrigu or attributed to him. But more than this we do not know. It is quite likely however that it was made at the instance of or under the auspices of a king who after troubled times sought to ascertain the lost laws. We know of such an attempt with reference to Manu's Code in Samudragupta's time and that it is to that monarch that we owe the existence of Manu in its present form. Whether that was the first compilation of Manu in the manner here suggested or whether before it a code of Manu had already been compiled present knowledge on the subject does not enable us to say.

The conclusions I have put forward above about the mode of compilation of Manu are undoubtedly of a tentative character. But that such a history of the Code is at least probable will not, I hope, be gainsaid. A comparison with the history of the Avesta, the sacred book of the Persians, would perhaps make the probability of my conclusion stronger. The original Avesta in the only two copies that existed of it was lost after Alexander's invasion. Fragments however were retained either in memory or in writing. These were collected by a Parthian King, named Valkhash and the extant original Zend-Avesta was compiled under Ardheshir by the high priest Tansar. It is clear from the work of Tansar that in making the compilation he did not merely collect and sort his materials but freely brought in his own contribution where he thought fit, and it is admitted by himself in his letter where he says "When Shahinshah wants to suppress any inquity of the Ancients which does not suit the necessities of the present, they say 'This is the old custom, it is the rule of the ancients.' Iniquity, past or present, is a thing to be reproved whether it comes from the ancients or from the moderns. But Shahinshah has authority over religion and God is his ally ; and in thus destroying and changing of the order of tyranny, I see him more armed and adorned with more virtues than the ancients" (j). This, Darmesteter rightly considers to be a confession that Tansar's "restoration is an adptation" (k). Manu's compiler may very well have done the same thing with Manu's texts and possibly impelled by the same motives.

The history of the *Zend-Avesta* likewise furnishes an analogy to the additions which I suppose to have been made in Manu, for we hear of Shahpuhr I. ordering the wisdom of the Avesta relating to the profane sciences scattered amongst the Hindus and Greeks to be collected and embodied in Tansar's text of the Avesta—a veiled confession, as Darmesteter takes it, of the fact that the Zend-Avesta was enriched by Shahpuhr by scientific materials gathered from Greek and Indian sources (l). Both the example and the fiction might well have been reproduced in the actual history of the Manu Samhita. This historical illustration coming from a race which had so much in common with ancient Indians certainly gives us an insight into the thoughts and feelings of ancient Indians which would enable us to interpret the motives which prompted the compilers of Manusamhita to proceed to the work, as well as the principles on which they carried it on. We know what a king would do in those days when the law was lost and there were a number of fragmentary works dividing people into various camps as there were in Persia in the days of Ardheshir. We know that it would be a learned Brahman who would naturally be called upon to restore the traditional old Code of Manu and we know that he would take the opportunity not only to enshrine in his compilation genuine texts of Manu but also to add to them his own texts from considerations of policy. The probability is all in favour of this view rather than that a brand new code was compiled and immediately passed muster under the revered name of Manu or even that a sutra Manu was rendered into verse with copious additions.

(j) Tansar's letter, quoted in Darmesteter's Zend-Avesta (Sacred Books of the East) Introd. p. xliv.

(k) Darmesteter *loc cit.*

(l) Darmesteter op cit p. xlvi.

The history of Yâjnavalkya's Code may have been similar. Luckily in this case we have no hypothesis drawn from a Yâjnavalkya charana, but all the same a hypothesis has been made that there was an old sutra work belonging to some charana of the Black Yajurvedis. This is straining theory to the breaking point. The facts however of which we can be reasonably sure is that Yâjanvalkya was a sage held in high esteem in Mithila from the Vedic times. There would naturally be a number of sayings and ordinances attributed to Yajnavalkya just as we have any number of slokas current under Kalidas's name and moral maxims attributed to Chânakya. It would be nothing unusual for a Maithilia king to have a compilation of Yâjnavalkya's laws to be made. While the respect which Yâjnavalkaya's name always commanded in Mithila would give such a work immediate authority, the work might very well have been very largely an adaptation of customary laws and sayings as well as of rules gathered from other works current amongst the people. It must be said however that this history would be entirely conjectural.

It is clear that at some period of Indian history there was quite a craze for such reconstructions. We have any number of Smritis going under the names of the traditional law-giving sages of India whose works were possibly lost. One of these works go under the name of Apastamba which a comparison with Apastamba's sutras would show to have had absolutely no connection with the original. It was perhaps compiled in a part of the country where Apastamba's genuine sutras had been long lost and the compiler felt himself at liberty to palm off anything as Apastamba's Smriti. This compilation alone throws discredit on the entire body of these mushroom Smritis. It is doubtful moreover whether these works ever attained any importance or authority. They have not much of it to-day and the fact that what we have of these are evidently mere fragments certainly tells against their having any authority at any time (*m*).

If we are correct in our conjecture about the nature and history of Manu's Smriti, Nelson's bold assumption that Manu was the law-giver of only an insignificant sect (*n*) would appear to be absurd. Even assuming that Manu's original work was the hand-book of a charana of the Maitrayaniyas, that would not of itself justify the hasty conclusion which he draws. For, there

---

(*m*) A number of these Smritis are collected in Manmatha Nath Datta's Dharmasastras.

(*n*) Nelson : Prospectus on a Scientific Study of Hindu Law Ch. II where Manu is described as "a non-descript manual of extinct Mânavas."

is nothing in the Charanavyuha which would militate against the assumption that the Mânava was representative of the parent charana and its Code the original Code upon the model of which all the others were composed. There is no evidence that it was so but this is at least conceivable. Now when one charana develops out of another it does not necessarily throw away the authority of the works and traditions of the parent charana. On the contrary, from what we have seen about the nature of their development we should expect the offsprings to show the most sedulous respect to the parent institution though in practice they may have made departures more or less important (*o*). So it might very well be that the original Manu representing the old stock prior to the break up of the various charanas would be held in high esteem by all charanas which in their turn purported to develop and not overide its law.

But the whole idea that the text books of the charanas were sectional authorities is apparently based on no authority. It is true that these Codes grew up in isolation from one another and separated from one another by space and time. But the laws which each propounded purported to be not the sacred laws of any particular charana but the sacred laws of the Aryas as settled by the tradition and custom of the Holy land and supported by the Smirti in its various Sâkhas. When they were composed their authority may have been limited in practice to the charana for which they were compiled ; and, we have seen, their authority at that time was not more than that due to a systematic treatment, by very learned men, of the sacred laws ;—but in theory the laws purported to be the eternal laws of the Aryas. The process of diversification of the sacred laws with the spread of the people over different parts of the country and the corresponding multiplication of text books was a natural one. It may have gone on quite unconsciously and without any desire on the part of anybody to expressly depart from old tradition. Each text book may have been a manual habitually referred to in a particular charana and thus gained authority in that particular charana. That would justify us in holding that they represented different sectional laws, as little as we should be justified in saying that the teachings of Labeo and Capito represented two different sects in Rome. The Hindu Jurists like Labeo and Capito and their followers took

(*o*) This would appear from the fact that a Dharma Sutra of a later charana never taken upon itself to criticise a tenet of a manual of an older Charana of the same Sâkha.

different views of the laws and customs but each purported to propound not parochial or sectional law but what was the sacred established law of the people. When the time for the integration of the various laws came by reason of the mixture of the various charanas and a spread of knowledge of all their various text books it was natural that each should be looked upon as laying down the sacred laws not of a sect but of the Aryas in general. It is as such that we find these authorities referred to everywhere. Moreover by the time that this integration took place, the transformation of these text books into sacred works called Smritis in the technical sense had been completed. They were now supposed to be authoritative works compiled by Vedic Rishis out of their supreme knowledge and there was no questioning the authority of any as limited to any sect or clan. If ever there were any local or sectional barriers in the laws they must have been swept away by the time that the new idea of Smriti represented in Manu's Code came into vogue. For the Codes of Manu, Yâjnavalkya and Parâsara contemplate the various Dharmasastras as being all alike authoritative as secondary revelation and not in any sect or clan but all over the Aryan world. These sages enumerate the authors of Dharmasâstras whose works are to have authority and some attempt is even made to settle their order of precedence in the manner of the Valentinian Law of Citations. We get it then that at the time of Manu and Yâjnavalkya there were no parochial or sectional codes of law but each code was viewed as of universal authority. The authority extended not in a general sort of way to the teachings of the sages but to the very letter of the law they laid down—an idea that is supported and developed in all the commentaries which refer to Smriti texts indifferently as of equal authority (*p*).

The transformation of Smriti into a technical term is as little surprising as the canonisation of the great teachers. What happened in India, happened also at Rome, with this difference that the spiritual pre-eminence accorded to the law-giving sages was unknown in Rome. Not that deification was unknown, for we find Emperors and even women alike Julia Augusta raised to divinity even in their life time, but the religious sanctity which the Roman mind would willingly associate with the head of the state

---

(*p*) Occasionally superior authority beinkg conceded to Manu on the authority of Brihaspati cited *ante*. Vijnaneswara says विरोधे तु विकल्पः in community on Yajnavalkya I 4—5 ,enumerating the authors of Dharmasastras.

was not accorded to her law-giver. That was because law in Rome had from a variety of causes shed its religious significance, while in India from quite another set of causes the religious element, with which law started in both countries, was intensified and emphasised, and law founded on a religious philosophy. Thus while the authority of the secularised law of Rome passed gradually to the people, the religious philosophy gave an opposite turn to the law in India and it passed entirely into the hands of a privileged class of specialists. To be in keeping with the religious origin of law it was necessary that the men who had practically acquired the power of making or moulding of law should acquire a high spiritual status. We find therefore that, wherever a law is received from human hands, divinity or divine inspiration must be imputed to him. The teachers of law must be semi-divine like Manu or great seers ; and, if the king makes laws, that must be because he had elements of the divine in him.

The nature of the authority which was accorded to Smriti naturally varies at different stages. In the Sutra Smritis the word implied merely traditions handed down from the sages and this had obviously a merely secondary authority, subject to the primary authority of sruti, although it enjoyed practical primacy (*q*). At a later stage, also represented in the Sutra Smritis, we find Sruti texts confronted with traditional rules thus threatening the practical primacy of the Smritis. In Manu's Code the testimony is ambiguous but the way in which Veda and Smriti are referred to by themselves as distinct from the other sources (*r*) suggested that the author was contemplating their equal authority. Jaimini, if we accept Sabaraswami's interpretation of his texts, gives to Smriti only secondary authority which would be displaced by the superior authority of Sruti (*s*). Kumarilaswami however demurs

---

(*q*) See *ante* p. 41.

(*r*) श्रुति स्मृत्युदितं धर्ममनुतिष्ठन् हि मानवः ।
इह कीर्त्तिमवाप्नोति प्रेत्यचानुत्तमं सुखम् ॥
श्रुतिस्तु वेदो विज्ञेयः धर्मशास्त्रं तु वै स्मृतिः ।
ते सर्व्वार्थेष्वमीमांस्ये ताभ्यां धर्मो हि निर्बभौ ॥ Manu II, 9—10.

Kulluka, commenting on the 1st passage says that this has been said

"स्मृतेः श्रुतितुल्यत्व बोधेनाचारादिभ्यो बलवत्त्वप्रतिपादनार्थं"

Medhatithi puts the same argument in the mouth of the Purvapaksha, but he too looks upon Smriti as more authoritative than **Achâra**.

(*s*) **Jaimini I, iii, 3** ***et seq*****.**

to this view of the Bhasyakara and holds that Smriti must be regarded as co-ordinate in authority with the Sruti (*t*).

This difference between Sabara and Kumarila is founded on a difference between them in their view of the nature of Smriti (*u*). In the view of Sabaraswami the Smritis are founded on vedic rules. There are some cases in which the original Vedic authorities for the Smriti rules can be traced, but in most cases they represent recollections by the sages of lost Vedic texts. As recollections they only raise a presumption of Vedic authority which is displaced by a Vedic text to the contrary. In this view Sabaraswami is supported by the authority of old Sutra writers like Apastamba.

Kumarilaswami on the other hand contends that the Smritis were not compilations by sages from their recollections of lost Vedic texts but primarily manuals collecting Vedic rules which were scattered about in the various Sâkhas compiled for the guidance of men (*v*). He would not admit that any rule of Smriti may have to be referred to lost Sruti (*w*). The Sâkhas of the Sruti are innumerable and no one can say that any rule is not to be found in any one of those Sâkhas. He holds therefore that the Smritis are compilations of Vedic precepts by the Rishis in their own words collected from various Sâkhas (*x*). Whenever you find any Smriti text you must suppose that it is based upon text of Sruti in one or the other of the innumerable Sâkhas. The presumption of Sruta origin would not be displaced altogether by a contrary Sruti. The more proper view would be to regard the Smriti text also as based on a Vedic text and thus to look upon the conflict as one between too contrary Srutis. So that in case

---

(*t*) Tantravarttika p. 105-6 (Benares Ed.)

वैदिकी हीदृश एवार्थः पुरुषैर्यः प्रकाश्यते ।
स पठद्भिः प्रकाश्येत स्मरद्भिर्वेति तुल्यभाक् ।
तेनार्थं कथयद्भिर्या स्मृतार्थं कथ्यते श्रुतिः ।
पठिताभिः समानोऽसौ केन न्यायेन बाध्यते ।

(*u*) See Bhasya and Varttika on Jaimini I, 3, ii, 3, et seq.

(*v*) शाखान्तरविप्रकीर्णानि हि पुरुषान्तरप्रत्यक्षाणि च वेदवाक्यानि पुरुषधर्मानुष्ठानकालेष्वपठितानि वेद॰ समाम्नाय विनाशभयात् स्वरूपेणानुपन्यस्यार्थोपनिबन्धद्वारेणभ्यानि विशिष्टधर्मिस्थानीयेन तेनैव परेणाप्यपि व्यज्यमानानि पिण्डीकृत्य ग्रथ्यन्ते ।

Tantravarttika (Benares Ed.) p. 105.

(*w*) Tantravarttika p. 115. (Benares Ed.)

(*x*) *Ibid.* p. 76.

of a conflict between Sruti and Smriti we must not give the go by to the Smriti but look upon the case as one of Vikalpa or option (*y*). That is the highest at which the authority of the Smriti has been put and it is difficult to say that any other commentator has gone so far as that. The more general opinion would seem to be in favour of Sabara's theory that a Smriti text is over riden by a contrary Sruti (*z*).

I have said before that the word Smriti is used in the later Dharmasutras and the commentaries in a technical sense. But even as such its derivative meaning was retained ; it was, in fact, what is called a Yogarurha or technical word founded on a derivative sense. The term is limited in its denotation to the works called Dharmasâstras but the authority of these was founded on the fact of their representing recollections of sages who are entitled to respect. This sense the term retains to this day.

When authors like Gautama, Baudhayana and Vasistha wrote, there was no occasion to specify whose Smriti or recollection of the law was entitled to respect. All that Gautama insists on is that it should be the recollection of persons who have the reputation of a thorough knowledge of the Veda. It is not clear whether he implied that the person whose recollection is to be treated as binding should himself be a seer or Rishi. By the time that the metrical Smritis were composed there must have been quite a number of works claiming authority as Smriti, so that Manu, Yâjnavalkya and Parasara found it necessary to enumerate the really authoritative Smritis (*a*). But they did nothing more than that. It would be those authors alone whose works would be entitled to authority and none others, they said ; but they did not say why they should have this preference accorded to them. The commentators generally proceed upon that enumeration alone without making any attempt to found their authority on any general principle. Kumarilaswami however traces the

---

(*y*) Referring to a case of supposed conflict between Vedic precept and Smriti Kumarila says,

विकल्प एव हि न्याय्यस्तुल्यकक्षप्रमाणतः । *op cit* p. 107.

(*z*) Kulluka in places (Manu II, 10 and II 14) holds that Sruti and Smriti are of equal authority. But he is not quite consistent in his opinion. Medhatithi after discussing the controversy between those who hold Smritis to be founded on destroyed texts and those who derive them from scattered texts in quisting sâkhas gives his opinion in favour of the latter, that is Kumarilaswami's view. But he does not stand out, all the same, for equal authority of Sruti and Smriti.

(*a*) See *ante* p. 42.

authority of Smritis to a general principle instead of basing its argument upon the mere enumeration.

This was called for by the growth of a class of works also called Smriti belonging to the Buddhists. These works were evidently so much in the public eye that Kumarila felt himself called upon to enter into an elaborate argument to show why these works should not be regarded as equally authoritative with the orthodox Smritis. In the course of this argument he lays down as a general principle that when Smritis are referred to as authority the recollection of those alone is meant who are referred to as Rishis in the Vedas. And it is upon this fact alone that the authority of their works is founded according to the learned author. These seers had visions of the Veda, they had the supreme knowledge. When they lay down anything as laid down in the Sruti which they have helped to make known, their opinion was surely entitled to authority. It is because the Veda and the Smriti are in a manner the work of the same men that they should alike command confidence. That is the argument which Kumarila puts forward. It is an illustration of the manner in which these later authors sought to derive the authority of the sources of law from the authority of the Vedas which was of course a fundamental fact (*b*).

In thus basing the authority of Smriti on the fact of the prophetic character of the authors Kumarila was not unhistorical nor was he starting quite a novel thesis. As a matter of fact his view is a more explicit statement and the logical completion of what the entire Smriti literature was apparently struggling to express. The tradition of Recollection being a source of law was well established. The underlying reason for this was the natural assumption that when a rule was stated to be law by one who knew all the Vedas he must have had authority for it in the Vedas. That is an assumption which we find running through the entire Smriti literature. But Kumarilaswami went beyond this underlying assumption when he insisted upon common authorship of the Vedas and Smritis as the foundation of the authority so that the authoritative propounders of the law must be not only men learned in the Vedas but seers themselves. He cannot quite be accused of going against history in taking Smriti in the technical sense, as that tradition must have been of quite a long standing by his time, but he was unhistorical in raising the Sutra writers to the rank of Rishis. We have seen before that

---

(*b*) See text cited at p. 3 *ante*.

Apastamba himself disclaims on behalf of avaras or latter day men all pretensions to the status of a seer (*c*). We can understand whom he means *avaras* if we remember that Svetaketu referred to in the Chandogya and Brihadaranyaka Upanishads is an example of these latter day men who can't be Rishis.

Kumarila's views on the nature of the authority of the Smritis must in these respects be considered more or less singular, for though they are generally accepted by Mimansists of to-day they are not as a rule followed by the commentators of the Smritis. They are content, as I have said before, with taking the enumerations as showing the authority of Smriti writers without attempting to find any ulterior principle under those enumerations, and they do not also generally question the power of an express Sruti text to override a rule of the Smriti.

But Kumarilaswami and the commentators on law are agreed on this that texts of the Smritis must be taken literally and every word of them would have to be accounted for. They were in fact a part of the *lex scripta* and had to be interpreted to the last word according to the ordinary canons of interpretation. It is acknowledged by all that Smritis do not reproduce the exact words of the Sruti. But at the same time, in the absence of Sruti texts it is not permissible to anybody to reject any portion of the rule in the Smritis. We must assume in fact not only that a Smriti text in a general sort of way expresses the sense of a Vedic text but that it does so completely.

So that in spite of the difference of opinion on cases of conflict, all authors agree that where a Smriti text is to be applied it had to be applied to the last letter as any Vedic text. But these texts had to be interpreted and the divergent texts of the various Smritis which were all recognised as having equal authority had to be harmonised For this purpose you had to apply to the texts of the Smriti the same rules of interpretation as you applied to the Sruti.

It was thus that raising of the Dharmasastras to the rank of the lex scripta brought in its wake its interpretation according to the rules of Vedic exegesis, that is, according to the rules and maxims of the Mimansa system. It is upon this manner of exegesis that the entire development of the Smriti law in the hands of the commentators from Medhatithi and Asahâva to Râghunandana and Sreekrishna Tarkalankara is founded.

So much for the general authority of Smritis. We shall be

(*c*) See p. 49 *ante*.

in a better position to appreciate the views on its comparative authority with reference to custom when we have dealt with that source of law.

§4. Sacred Custom.

As has been observed before, tradition and custom were the twin sources of sacred law in ancient India. With advent of the Sruti theory these were made secondary sources. But in the earliest available texts on the subject we find but little effort to discriminate between custom and Smriti far from placing Smriti over custom.

The earliest records on the subject seem, according to Max Müller's understanding of the texts, (*d*) to place the Kalpasutras in a position secondary to that of customs. The Grihya sutras according to this view would be merely attempts to compile rules of general application only, which would be liable to be overriden by any custom prevailing in the Sâkha or Kula. The Dharmasutras which apparently followed the general plan of the Srauta and Grihya Sutras in this respect would in this view also appear to have been originally directed towards the object of laying down rules of general application only, leaving intact the customs of Kulas and other societies.

Of this at any rate we may be sure that the Dharmasutras leave ample scope open to family or other customs and the only limitation that they lay down to their applicability is that they should not be opposed to the Sruti (*e*). No claim is anywhere made in these works to override such customs merely because they are opposed to the Dharmasastras or the traditions they represent.

It is not in respect of family class or local customs alone that the Smritis recognise the authority of usage. On general laws

---

(*d*) Max Müller (op cit p. 52) cites the following text from the Aswalâyana Grihya Sutras : "अथ खलूच्चावचा जानपद धर्मा ग्रामधर्माश्च तान्विवाहे प्रतीयाद्यत्तु समानं तद्वक्ष्याम: which he translates as follows : "Now the customs of countries and places are certainly mainfold. One must know them as far as marriage is concerned. But we shall explain what is general custom." The commentator however gives a meaning entirely different. He says : जानपदादि धर्माणां वक्ष्यमाणानां धर्माणां च विरोधे सति वक्ष्यमाणं धर्ममेव कुर्यान्न जनपदादि धर्ममिति । यद्वक्ष्यामस्तत् सर्व्वत्रसमान मित्यर्थ: ।

(*e*) The only qualification given are "तुल्यभावे," Vasistha I, 7 ; "चाम्नायैरविरुद्धा:" Gautama, X, 20 ; and other places.

too, customs are referred to, though we find the scope of custom getting more and more restricted as we go, say from the Grihya sutras to commentators like Kulluka. On this matter there seems to exist some amount of confusion owing to a failure to distinguish between different grades of custom and the scope and degrees of authority recognised for each.

The Smriti texts relating to the authority of custom appear to recognise four different kinds of usage ; viz., (1) Kulâchara, (2) the practices of eminent sages, (3) the customs of good people, and (4) secular customs, specially those appertaining to low castes, heretic sects and the like. Of these, Kulâchara or the custom of the Kulas is partly religious and partly secular. The practice of eminent sages or spiritual leaders of men as well as the practices prevailing among good men generally are sources of Dharma. The last class, however, are customs which the king is advised to recognise though they do not appertain to the religious law. Much harm has been done by the failure in judicial and scientific discussions to recognise these different classes of customary law.

As I have mentioned before, the Grihya sutras seem to indicate the first attempts to generalise the religious observances of the various Kulas. Prior to that, the religious observances as well as the laws of people were evidently regulated largely by customs of the gens supplemented by instructions on points of difficulty from the Parishads. The Dharmasutras represent a further movement in the same direction, and in these works we find the generalisation of the law pretty far advanced. Ample scope is, however, still reserved to the Kuladharma, subject to the reservation, based on the Sruti theory, that it must not be opposed to the Sruti.

Such a limitation on the authority of the customs of the family was quite natural, once you begin to look upon Sruti as embracing the sum total of knowledge. For, as I have observed before, in the infancy of society, so soon as habit springs into self-consciousness it is found clothed with a spiritual character and is obeyed from religious instincts at least as much as from habit. When therefore the religious ideas of the people were integrated into the notion of the unity of religion and law symbolised in the Sruti theory, it could not but be that the sanctity of family custom must yield place, in theory at least, to the authority of Sruti. It is difficult to believe, however, that that would have made any very great difference in practice at the outset. One would rather expect that people would continue to cling to their family customs subject to the recognition of the supremacy of the Sruti, and it was not likely that their faith in the former would be too much interfered with at the start by a constant confronting of them with the Sruti. That was to come at a later time when the roots of the people's faith in their family customs had become much looser, and the Sruti theory, followed up by a general study of available Srutis, was far more developed in authority and strength. But the germ of the disintegration of family custom, as of the other classes of custom, by the authority of the sacred law lay in this, to the contemporaries apparently immaterial, recognition of the authority of Sruti. The mode in which this disintegration was effected we shall see when we come to the other general sacred customs.

I have spoken of Kuladharma, but all the authorities from Gautama to Yajnavalkya couple with it the *dharma* of the countries and the classes (jatis) as on the same footing (*f*). Jati does not, it should be noted here, mean castes, at any rate, the four broad classes of men which are primarily meant by caste, but rather smaller groups of men falling under one or other of the groups possibly united by a notion of common origin. In the commentaries we find *Jati* distinguished from *varna,* as implying the mixed castes and communities outside the four *varnas*. I am inclined to understand the term as used in the Smritis generally to imply any permanent association of men belonging to a common persuasion or calling, including the smaller communities which must have existed within the four broad classes. At any rate, this is clear that by jati-dharma is not meant the Dharma of the four principal castes or varnas. This was entirely regulated by the sacred law, evidently because the classes were themselves but a creation of that law and had no existence as such, apart from the various natural groups which went to make them up and therefore had no customary rules which might demand adjustment to the sacred law.

By *desa*-dharma is understood the custom of a country, with this reservation, however, that it must be Dharma or religious custom. It is perfectly clear that by this term the Aryan compilers of law must have contemplated the customs of the clean classes—the true Aryas alone. The custom of inferior classes of Sudras, Nishâdas, Chandalas and Swapâks, they were not con-

(*f*) Gautama XI, 20. Apastamba II, 6, 15, 1. Manu VIII, 41, 46 (in the former Manu mentions श्रेणीधर्मं as well and without the qualification 'unopposed to Sruti' as in the latter texts) Vasistha I, 17.

cerned with in this connection. They could not possibly conceive of the customs of these people as Dharma though perhaps these must be suffered to exist; for nothing could be more intolerable than that Chandâlas and Swapâks should affect to follow the sacred law (*g*). In reading the discourses of the various authors on Indian law, it is of importance to bear in mind the broad fissure which ran through society all over India between the clean and unclean classes, or in other words, between the Arya and non-Arya. When an early author like Baudhâyana, or a late one like Medhâtithi or Kumarilaswami begins to discant on the customs of various countries, we should be grievously misjudging them if we did not remember that they were not talking of the customs of Chandalas or even of Sudras, but only of Brahmans and the clean classes, and laying down their obligatory character for those classes alone. That this alone could have been meant is made clear by Apastamba, according to whom customs prevailing amongst the three upper castes alone are to be followed as Dharma, and that because these raise a presumption of a Srauta origin for them. Of this presumption we shall hear more presently (*h*).

The second broad class of customary law I have mentioned before is what is called by the Smriti writers the *Sila* of those who know the Vedas. Gautama refers to the Smriti (recollection) and the *Sila* (practices) of men who know the Vedas, as authorities for law, in the same breath (*i*). The authority for both these classes of law was apparently founded by Gautama on the same presumption, viz., that those who knew the Vedas so well must in the one case have laid down a rule, and in the other acted in their own life according to the dictates of the Sruti, though we may not be in a position now to trace the particular text upon which the teaching or the practice was based. As sources of law,

---

(*g*) This would be clear on a reference to the texts, some of which are referred to in the last note, which require the *desadharma* to be followed in that particular country without any limitation as to caste. It would be absurd, however, to suppose that the Smritis required a small colony of Brahmans settled amongst a population of Chandâlas to follow the customs of these people which would be the *desadharma* in the strictly literal sense of term.

(*h*) Apastamba II, 29, 14. Elsewhere he speaks of "what Aryas praise" meaning by Aryas of course the upper classes, also I, 12, 10. On the meaning of Dharma and the kinds of it dealt with in the Smritis, see Mitakshara under I, 1, Dharma is distinguished from *artha, kâma, moksha*. On the applicability of Smritis pre-eminently to dwijas alone.

(*i*) Gautama I, 2, 3 वेदोधर्ममूलं तद्विदाञ्च स्मृतिशीले ।

therefore, *Smriti* and *Sila* of these men stood on the same footing. We are cautioned, however, to be circumspect in inferring a rule of conduct from Sila ; for the seers were after all men, and their earthly passions might well have got the better of their religious discipline. We can, therefore, infer any conduct of the sages as based on the sacred law only when he clearly acts not from any obvious earthly motives but with a pure desire to conform to the law (*j*).

Vasistha and Baudhâyana apply almost the same tests, but on a more elaborate scale, to the source of law which they call Sishtâchâra or the practices of *Sishtas*. There would seem to be little doubt that those authors are refering in this to the same source that Gautama calls the *Sila* of those who know the law. While Gautama, however, names as his exemplars "those who know the Vedas," Vasistha and Baudhayana call them *Sishtas*. A Sishta is defined by Vasistha as a man "whose heart is free from desire" (*k*). Baudhayana understands by *Sishtas* those "who are free from envy, free from pride, contented with a store of grain sufficient for ten days, free from covetousness and free from hypocrisy, arrogance, greed, perplexity and anger, who in accordance with the sacred law have studied the Veda together with its appendages, know how to draw inferences from that and are able to adduce proofs perceptible by the senses from the revealed texts" (*l*) which is merely an elaboration of Vasistha's conception.

We have observed before that it is not quite clear whom Gautama understood by "those who know the Veda". If he meant to restrict the term to seers, his position would seem to be a strict logical deduction from the Sruti theory. On the other hand, he may have meant merely eminent Vedic scholars who have lived a pure life. The former seems to be a more probable view. In that case Vasistha and Baudhâyana may be taken to have extended the scope of this source of law by replacing "seers" by sages with less transcendent pretensions. We have seen, however, that they as well as Gautama and Apastamba place the same limitation on our liberty to draw a rule of conduct from the practice of sages, viz., that the practice must not be founded on any obvious worldly motives but must have been due to a pure desire to conform to the law.

(*j*) दृष्टोधर्मव्यतिक्रमः साहसञ्च महतां, न तु दृष्टार्थोऽवरदौर्बल्यात्। Gautama 1, 3.

(*k*) **Vasistha i, 6.**

(*l*) **Baudhâyana I, 1, 5.**

We shall presently see that at later times, or at any rate by other authors, the scope of this sort of custom has been widened and they refer not to the practices of sages of such spiritual eminence alone, but to all customs prevailing amongst good Aryas as authoritative, subject to the same limitation, viz., that they must not have been due to any worldly motives. It is clear that the recognition of the authority of such customs must have stood on the same footing as that of the *Sila* of spiritual leaders, and that very probably the two classes of usage were but different moments in the development of the same idea. The development itself must have been directed by the gradual approximation of the Sruti theory to the fact of the authority of custom ;—the Dharmasastras were really striving to integrate the two notions of the fundamental religious authority of law and the practical authority of custom. The synthesis that was finally arrived at was midway between the two.

But so far as the texts went, there was a clear discrepancy as to the real nature and source of authority of customary law. Was it limited to illustrious precedents of the type referred to by Gautama, or did the authority extend to practices of Aryas generally as Apastamba contends? In the latter case, Gautama's text would be superfluous. An attempt appears to have been made to reconcile the two views by Manu who refers to the *Sila* of those who know the Veda and the âchara of good men as distinct sources of law. In so doing he seems to include the rule of Vasistha and Baudhâyana along with customs of all Aryans under the latter, while Gautama's source is referred to the former. Evidently he understands *Sila* here in a different sense from the obvious meaning of Gautama. We get a clue to the true meaning that Manu attaches to *Sila* in the following text of Hârita cited by Kulluka:

"True Brahmanical character, devotion to gods and parents (or pitris), good temper, freedom from regret and jealousy, mildness, want of rudeness (and violence), friendliness, fair speaking, gratitude, kindness to those who seek protection, pity, calmness, these are the thirteen kinds of *Sila*" (*n*).

(*m*) Manu II, 10.

(*n*) ब्रह्मण्यता देवपितृभक्तता सौम्यताऽपरितापिताऽनसूयता मृदुताऽपारुष्यं मैत्रता प्रियवादित्वं कृतज्ञता शरण्यता कारुण्यं प्रशान्तिश्चेति त्रयोदशविधं शीलम्।

Hârita quoted by Kulluka. Kulluka also cites Govindaraja as explaining शील as रागद्वेषादिपरित्याग Sarvajnanârayana understands by शील,

Medhatithi too, in the conflicting arguments by means of which he elaborates his exposition, gives several possible meanings of *Sila.* Manu must have had some such special meaning of *Sila* in mind when he set it up as an authority for law as distinct from custom of good men. That possibly was a device for getting rid of the stringent limitation which Gautama had put on the nature of this source of law. For if that was the only kind of practice which could become a source of general law, would be practically a denial of the possibility of customary sacred law of general application.

Of far greater importance is general custom, not practices of saints and seers, but such as prevails amongst Aryan peoples. Such custom is sacred, and any practice based on it would lead to religious merit, provided that it was not one which men would naturally evolve if they followed but their natural inclinations. It is such customs on which the elders of the society referred to by Gautama could advise. Apastamba clearly places the authority of such customs on the hypothesis of their raising a presumption of foundation on Vedic law. This conception was the result of the integration of the Sruti theory with the authority of customs in fact. It would seem however that the presumption of Vedic origin raised by them was derived historically from the authority which properly appertained to practices of persons of spiritual eminence. It is to these that the presumption would primarily apply ; at a later stage of thought the same presumption would be requisitioned in aid of approved customs of the Aryans generally.

It is such general customs that are referred to by Apastamba, Manu and Yajnavalkya (*o*). Though they do not say so, they obviously contemplate them from the same point of view as Apastamba, whose opinion was really the orthodox opinion we find enshrined in Jaimini's Mimansa (*p*) and was apparently founded on a fairly old tradition.

चित्तस्य स्वभावप्रथया while Raghavananda gives वृत्तं, चरित्रं as a meaning of शील as an alternative to the one suggested by Kulluka. Medhatithi understands समाधि by शील। He implies evidently that the absolute knowledge which sages gain in the state of Samâdhi is a source of law which is here meant.

(*o*) Apastamba I, 12, 10 ; II, 29, 14 ; I, 20, 8. Yajnavalkya I, 7 ; Manu II, 12.

(*p*) I iii 5—7.

The effect of the presumption on the authority of custom was to make it of secondary importance to the Sruti. If custom was authoritative solely because it was presumably founded on the Sruti, its authority would be wholly displaced by a contrary Sruti text. And that is the law as we find it laid down by Apastamba. Here also Apastamba is clearly following the Mimansa view which is certainly not challenged by the other Smritis. In the Mimansa the theory of presumption is developed into a science, and we are told not only the conditions which would enable us to make the presumption, but are almost given the words in which the underlying Sruti text must be presumed. Thus for instance we must not presume more of Sruti than is absolutely necessary to justify the custom, and when we have a customary rule limited to a particular area we must not suppose the Vedic rule to be limited with reference to the area but to be of general application (*q*).

As to the exact nature of the authority of Sishtâchâra and its relation to the authority of Veda and Smriti there is some diversity of opinion among different law-givers and commentators. There are differences with reference to the exact usages which can claim authority, and the nature of the presumption raised by them as well as with reference to their relative authority as compared with Sruti and Smriti.

We have noticed above some of the differences on the first of these heads. While we find, generally speaking, a broadening of the law as to whose usages should be regarded as binding, as we come from Gautama to Manu and Yajnavalkya, we find, on the other hand, a retrograde tendency in most commentators. Thus while Manu speaks of good custom or "custom of good men" without reservation, Kumarilaswami would insist upon their being custom of *Sishtas*, and by "Sishtas" he understands those who have regulated their lives according to the dictates of the Vedas. The conduct even of these cannot be cited as precedent where it is prompted by worldly motives ; it must have been prompted by an *opinio necessitatis* and directed to supernatural ends. In this he agrees with the Bhâsyakara (*r*).

Medhâtithi understands good custom as *Sishtâchâra* but by Sishta he means merely those who know the Veda. Evidently he

(*q*) See Kishori Lal Sarkar's Tagore Law Lectures pp. 240 *et seq*, also p 254 *et seq* where he explains the well known Holakadhikarana. Jaimini I, iii, 15 *et seq*.

(*r*) Tantravârttika p. 131 यत् * * धर्मबुद्ध्याकुर्वन्ति तदपि सम्यक्त्वाद्धर्मरूपमेव।

is not referring to seers. Nor does he apparently require any extraordinary spiritual pre-eminence in those whose customs are to be followed. This would be clear if we refer to the illustrations of custom that he gives. These relate mostly to unimportant details in social and religious functions, such as marriage on which there is a great diversity of customs. On these small matters it requires no great spiritual eminence to advise. Sarvajnanârayana however defines good men as those who are engaged in acting according to the Veda. And by achara he understands not practice *per se*, but only practices which seek to follow practices of previous good men. That implies that no *Sadhu* or *Sishta* is competent to initiate a new practice on his own account ; his practices are only authoritative when he is himself simply seeking to pursue a course of conduct following that of good men of past times. Kulluka simply explains "good custom" as practices of Sishtas, but it is obvious he contemplates by it merely matters of a very trifling character, for he illustrates achara by saying "such as the use of blankets and bark-garments" (*s*).

Generally speaking therefore there was a tendency to whittle down the authority of custom in these various commentaries, either by demanding a too rigorous test for the âchâra or by regarding it as applicable within a very restricted sphere. That was natural when they had in hand elaborate works on sacred law like Manu, Vishnu and Yajnavalkya and when there were so many authoritative Smritis with co-ordinate authority which could be relied upon to furnish between them a text for every possible function having any religious bearing.

There is a general agreement amongst commentators, and there appears to be an assumption explicit or tacit in the Smritis that custom is presumably founded on some text of Sruti. That was likewise the foundation, as we have seen, of the authority of the Smriti. In either case express Sruti would therefore override their law. As we have seen however Smriti gained in authority with time and we find Kumarilaswami and Kullukabhatta boldly standing out for the equal authority of Sruti and Smriti. Their claim is also greatly supported by the texts of Manu which speak of Veda and Smriti apart from the other sources of law as the foundations of Dharma. Custom however not only never attained to that rank and dignity but appears to sink in authority, firstly by the application of some rigorous rules as to presumption of

(*s*) See under Manu II, 10.

Vedic authority from them, and partly by their being made subsidiary to Smritis as they always were to the Sruti.

Now in the older Smritis the only limitation that we find placed upon the authority of custom is that it should not be opposed to the Sruti. Baudhâyana and Vasistha no doubt refer to Sistâchara as a source of law only on the failure of Smriti, but at other places they only insist that a custom should not be opposed to Sruti. And if, as I suppose, they did not understand their own works by Smriti, it would be obvious that they did not necessarily imply that a custom opposed to the law they lay down would be bad. In Manu however we find that Smriti is understood as implying a body of written works, and they are raised to a position of equality with the Vedas. That was a sign that custom was sinking in importance as compared with the Smriti and the general opinion of commentators would seem to be that a sacred custom is of no authority if it is opposed to the Smriti though there are authors like Madhavacharyya and Nilakantha who stand out for the authority of customs opposed to the Smriti (*t*).

While thus sinking in theoretical authority, custom naturally continued in practice to have a determining influence upon the further development of law. This influence was however of an entirely indirect character. It produced great changes in the practical laws of the Aryas in different parts of the country, and there is no reason why the commentaries and Nibandhas should differ so much on a variety of topics unless it was on account of the variety of customs in the atmosphere of which they had grown up. If custom could not claim direct recognition as

---

(*t*) Narada I, 40 धर्मशास्त्रविरोधे तु युक्तियुक्तो विधिः स्मृतः। व्यवहारो हि बलवान् धर्मस्तेनावहीयते॥ places *Vyavahâra* above *dharma*. Asahaya understands by *Vyavahâra* customs of the people, but he takes Narada's text as implying simply that a law of the Smritis, such as for instance the one relating to remarriage of widows, Niyoga etc. is nevertheless not to be followed if it is disapproved by custom. This is a generally accepted opinion amongst commentators. But it is just possible that in this text as well as the previous one relating to *arthasastra* and *dharmasastra* (I, 39) Narada was simply dealing with the relative authority of rules laid down in different portions of the Smritis. The portion dealing with *arthasastric* rules such as the constitution of the administration would be inferior to those dealing with dharmasastra or religious law. That is how the Mitakshara understands the analogous text of Yajnavalkya (II, 21.) On the same principles we might say that Narada means to lay down that the vyavahara portions of the Smritis overrides the portion dealing merely with dharma.

such, it always came in under the guise of an interpretation of the sacred law. It was upon the diversities of custom, that are due the differences between the Mitakshara and the Dayabhaga on the nature of son's interests in the property in the hands of the father, on the powers of women to dispose of property, as well as those between the Vyavahara Mayukha and the other works on the capacity of women in all matters. The authors tried, as best they could, to deduce the customs which they found dominant in their own society from the authority of Sruti and Smriti, but what they practically did was really to give their support to a custom.

Moreover, although the sphere of custom as creating a rule of law was restricted, its abrogative function was clearly developing fast. It was quite natural that it should be so, for, in the absence of any effective repealing agency, custom was bound to be relied upon to get rid of obsolete texts. When Vijnanesvara lays down that a Dharma which is condemned by people should not be followed (*u*), we can assume that he was explicitly stating what is tacitly accepted by all.

We should be on our guard also from too readily assuming that custom was in fact sinking in authority as fast as some of the commentaries would have us believe. On the other hand, these commentaries, written mostly at a time when the character of Hindu law as positive law was on the wane, were in many matters divorced from actual facts and tended to develop too much of a scholastic tendency. We should not be surprised, therefore, to find that although vigorous attempts are made to whittle down the scope of custom, its actual sphere was not quite as narrow. Indications of this are furnished by the facts that some of the commentaries claim a far larger scope for custom than the more orthodox school would allow. Even Kumarilaswami gives a hint of the same fact by some of his alternative interpretations to Jaimini's Adhikarana on custom. Thus one of the interpretations recognises a custom as such as valid, not if it is one of the Sishtas, but if it is not forbidden or disapproved by Sishtas (*v*). So also when he reads the Adhikarana as consisting

---

(*u*) अस्वर्ग्यं लोकविद्विष्टं धर्म्ममप्याचरेन्नतु Cited by Vijnaneswara p. 180. So too Narada I, 40, according to Asahâya's interpretation upholds the paramount abrogative authority of custom.

(*v*) Tantravarttika (Benares ed) p. 145

शिष्टं यावत् श्रुतिस्मृत्योर्लोके यन्न विरुध्यते । तच्छिष्टाचरणं धर्म्मे प्रमाणत्वेन गम्यते ॥

यदि शिष्टस्य कोपः स्याद्विरुध्यते प्रमाणता । तदकोपात्तु नाचारः प्रमाणत्वं विरुध्यते ॥

of two parts, the second of which allows custom as such on mere worldly matters, keeping all restrictions for matters of sacrament and ritual, he is really recognising the inevitable authority of custom on most mundane matters, no matter of what character.

The authorities are not quite agreed as to the countries whose customs are to be regarded as good and capable of being counted for purposes of Dharma. Vasistha, Baudhâyana, Apastamba, Vishnu, Yajnavalkya and Manu, all give tables of countries which are to be counted as sacred and whose customs are to be counted as *sadâchara* or good custom (*w*). These enumerations are of no small importance historically, not merely to show the seats and centres of Aryan civilisation in the various ages but also to show the exact local scope of the sacred law. It is too often taken for granted that the Smriti law was the general law all over the vast continent of India. The Smriti writers themselves, however, point to a contrary conclusion by these enumerations of countries where clean customs prevail. That was the country of Arya law ; it was to this country—the Aryavarta—alone that the Smriti law was contemplated as applying.

Manu says that the customs, for instance, of Brahmavarta and Aryavarta should be followed (*x*). He means of course that they are to be followed only by Aryas of the holy countries and not that the Anaryas, Vrishalas and Vratyas of other countries are also to follow those laws. Yajnavalkya too makes it clear that the law he lays down is that of the country where the black antelope lives, i.e. of Aryavarta (*y*). It is true that Vasistha says that the *Dharma* and *achara* of Aryavarta must be *every where* acknowledged (*z*), but one has to read 'everywhere' as implying where Aryas live.

It is perfectly clear therefore that the Smritis do not contemplate their laws as applying to all the world but only to the elect people, the Aryas, living, in those times, in locally limited communities. In other countries, where Aryas did not live, the laws and customs might be otherwise.

That is the presupposition underlying all the Smritis and all commentaries more or less. The law they lay down is the *dharma* of the Aryas founded on the Sruti which was specially for the benefit of the Aryas. There might be customs which prevailed amongst non-Aryans, amongst Vratyas and Vrishalas, and they must needs be content with following them, but they would not be *dharma*. The only *dharma* is that of the Aryas and it is

(*w*) For instance Baudh. I, 2, 9—14. (*x*) II, 17 *et seq*. (*y*) I, 2. (*z*) I, 10.

to them alone that the laws of the Smriti apply. None else have the capacity for dharma or sacred law. We shall pursue the bearings of this fundamental fact on the practical laws of the country at a later stage of this thesis.

§5 Sruti, Smriti and Good Custom.

In the foregoing account of these sources of law I have incidentally noticed the relations of Sruti, Smriti and Achâra in Hindu legal theory, and I have also noted the distinctions between different Smriti writers and commentators on the scope to be assigned to each. I shall here briefly summarise my conclusions on this subject.

The Sruti from being originally a mere theoretical foundation of law has risen to the position of a practical source of sacred law, and as such its authority is undisputedly supreme. It had undoubted authority to override custom from the very earliest times. According to the general opinion it has authority also to override Smriti. Manu, however, appears to have made Sruti and Smriti co-ordinate authorities, and Kulluka and Kumarilaswami have worked up this theory to the logical conclusion that where there is a conflict between Sruti and Smriti it is to be read as a case of vikalpa where either course may be pursued.

We have seen the original nature of the Smriti and the extent of its authority in the Dharmasutras. At a later date, we find the Dharmasastras themselves raised to the dignity of Smriti and the meaning of the word restricted to them alone. These works inherit all the authority of the Smriti as understood by Gautama. We find, therefore, that Smriti is paramount authority subject to the authority of the Veda. At a certain stage of the development of the conception we find attempts made to ascertain the authors whose works are entitled to authority, possibly on account of the claims made by the Bauddhas on behalf of their own Smritis. The conclusion that Kumarila comes to on that point is that the Rishis whose works have authority as Smriti must be those spoken of as such by the Vedas. The result of such a conception of the authorship of the Dharma sutras was that they were raised almost to the same rank as the Vedas themselves, and we find Kumarila and Kulluka refusing to accept the position of Sabaraswami that a Smriti rule must yield to the superior authority of a Vedic precept.

By this time the authority of Smriti over custom has been completely established. Custom is from the very outset counted authoritative solely by virtue of its raising a presumption of Srauta origin. It can therefore be of no avail if it is against the express text of the Sruti. This idea leads to stringent limitations being placed on usage as a source of law. It has to be the usage of sages who know the Vedas. According to others again, it may be the usage of persons who have attained the status of a Sishta by acting according to the Vedas. In either case the practice must have been one prompted by the sole desire to act according to law and not ascribable to any worldly motives. In all this there is no reference to general custom.

General custom was, however, recognised from the earliest times, and Apastamba seems to speak of all approved customs without exception as raising a presumption of being founded on the Veda. We find a similar recognition of general custom in Manu, Yajnavalkya and Narada who call it Sadâchara, the *achara* of good men. Sadâchara is explained by Manu himself as denoting whatever custom prevails in Brahmavarta amongst the Varnas and the mixed castes. Medhâtithi in commenting upon this text makes his opponent say that, from this, a custom would be law irrespective of the knowledge of the Veda and the Sishtatwa of those who practice it (*a*). This argument is undoubtedly sound, and Medhatithi can only get round it by saying that this rule is laid down for Brahmâvarta because it may be presumed to be inhabited by Sishtas.

This general custom was subject apparently to the usual limitation that it must be unopposed to the Sruti. So much we get from Apastamba himself. The same limitation also applies to customs of countries, kulas, etc., so far as they are sacred.

In these cases, as well as in the case of the general customs referred to above, the presumption of Vedic origin is considerably weaker than in the case of Sishtâchara in the strict sense of the term. But Kumarilaswami, in one of the alternative interpretations to the Adhikarana on custom, extends the presumption to these customs also. The presumption arises according to this view from the fact that it is not disapproved by Sishtas.

This extension of the patronage of Sruti gives to these customs a footing which they would not otherwise have ; but at the same time it places a limitation upon the scope of custom which we find uniformly insisted on by the commentaries, viz., that it must be unopposed not merely to the Sruti, as the Smritis themselves lay down, but also to the Smritis or Dharmasastras. For the

(*a*) Under Manu II, 18.

authors of Dharmasastras are undoubtedly Sishtas, and if they condemn a custom, that rebuts the presumption of Srauta origin which can only arise from non-condemnation by Sishtas. That is how Kumarilaswami interprets Jaimini (*b*). Medhatithi arrives at the same conclusion by a different argument. Achara of this kind, according to him, can only lead to the presumption of its being founded on Smriti, and from Smriti again Sruti is to be presumed. Smriti, on the other hand, raises a direct presumption of Sruti. Hence Smriti is to be preferred to Achara (*c*). Medhatithi gives no authority for this apparently novel law of presumption, but it would seem that at his time this view would receive acceptance without much argument.

Kulluka founds his conclusion as to the superior authority of Smriti upon his theory that Sruti and Smriti are to be looked upon as on an equal footing as sources of law (*d*). This conclusion he draws from the fact that Manu in some of his texts mentions Sruti and Smriti as distinguished from Achara and others as authorities for law *par excellence*. That, according to Kulluka, establishes the equality of Sruti and Smriti and the superiority of either to custom. That conclusion would also seem to follow from Vasistha's text who refers to Sishtâchara as authority only where Sruti and Smriti fail, though we can not be sure in what exact sense Vasistha uses the term Smriti.

With one or two exceptions all commentators and Nibandha writers are agreed that Smriti must have precedence over custom. A distinction must however be made between positive and negative precepts. Positive precepts of even the Sruti can be overruled by a negative custom, though negative precepts of the Smritis must have precedence over custom. That is the position which sacred custom holds in the mature jurisprudence of the Hindus.

§6 The King as a Source of Law.

The King as a legislator is not an idea congenial to the Aryan mind. "Among Aryan peoples" says Miraglia "there has never arisen that all-controlling despotism which blots out man, as in Egypt, Babylon, China, among the Mussalmans and the Tartar Tribes—or if it has appeared it has not been of long duration." (*e*). They were wedded to the ideas of autonomy and qualified theocracy embodied in their various communal groups and in the

(*b*) Tantravarttika cited *ante* p. 74..

(*c*) Under Manu II, 18.

(*d*) Under Manu II, 10.

(*e*) Miraglia: Comparative Legal Philosophy p. 120.

colleges of philosophical priests. Law was with them either sacred or profane. If it was the former, it was for the philosopher to expound it ; if it was the latter, it was for their community to lay it down.

So, although we hear a great deal of the various sacred sources of law and also of the authority of Corporations to govern their own affairs, we hear very little of the King as legislator. The only notable instance in which the King is mentioned as laying down the law occurs in a single passage of Manu, which, according to Medhatithi's interpretation, lays upon the subjects and officers the obligation of obeying whatever duty (Dharma) the King imposes by proclamation (*f*).

Coming after passages which extol the King as made up of Divine essence, this text surely seems to bear the meaning that Medhatithi assigns to it and gives to the King powers to legislate. Medhatithi reads into this power the limitation that the laws of the King are to be unopposed to not only the Sastras (including Smriti, Sruti, Purana, etc.) but also to the customs. Further such rules are to relate to secular matters alone. Sarvajnanarayana insists that this does not also authorise the King to make any new rule as to punishments, for the scale of punishments is fixed by law. These limitations are not to be found in the text, but they must, at the same time, be accepted as some of the unsaid presuppositions of this legal precept, which we have to supply from what we know about the ideas of the people and the constitution of the society. For if there is one thing more than any other that strikes us in Indian society at all ages, it is the tenacity with which the people cling to their traditional and sacred laws and

---

(*f*) तस्माद्धर्मं यमिष्टेषु स व्यवस्येन्नराधिपः ।
अनिष्टं चाप्यनिष्टेषु तं धर्म्मं न विचालयेत् ॥ Manu VII, 13.

Medhatithi comments on it as follows :—यतः सर्व्वतेजोमयो राजा तस्मात्तेनेष्टेषु वल्लभेषु मन्त्रीपुरोहितादिषु कार्य्यगत्या धर्म्मं कार्य्यव्यवस्थां शास्त्राचाराविरुद्धां व्यवसेन्निश्चित्य स्थापयेन्न विचालयेत्। सा तादृशी राज्ञोऽनुज्ञा नातिक्रमणीया। अद्य पुरे सर्व्वैरुत्सवः कर्त्तव्यः मन्त्रीगेहे विवाहो वर्त्तते तत्र सर्व्वैः सन्निधातव्यं तथा पशवो नाद्य सैनिकैर्हन्तव्याः न शकुनयोऽन्वेषयितव्याः नर्त्तकी धनिकैराराधणीया एतावन्त्यहानि। एवं अनिष्टेष्वपि एतेन संसर्गो न कर्त्तव्य एतस्य गृहे प्रवेशो न देयः एवंविधो धर्म्म पटहघोषादिना राज्ञादिष्टो नातिक्रमणीयः। नत्वग्निहोत्रादि धर्म्मव्यवस्थायै वर्णाश्रमिणां राजा प्रभवति।
But different interpretations are given by others. Burnell for instance follows that of Raghavananda in translating the passage thus : "Therefore let the King never alter the rule, either the law he arranges for those he loves or the punishment for those he dislikes."

customs. Each man was primarily bound up with the little society within the State to which he belonged and only indirectly felt or recognised the authority of the King. With such a constitution of society, it was not possible for a King to legislate in flagrant opposition to the traditions and usages. It would be apparent that the commands directed to the officers would be the earliest instances of royal legislative powers. Such commands were indispensable for the proper carrying out of the administration of the country and must have been tacitly recognised long before Manu thought of making them explicit law. It was a further extension of power that gave to the King the authority to give general commands apart from administrative rules.

Yajnavalkya takes the legislative powers of the King for granted when he speaks of the laws which should prevail in any corporation. There apparently he gives to King-made laws an authority secondary to what he calls *nijadharma,* presumably meaning thereby the law of the Sastras (*g*). It is noticeable that in other places where he speaks of general laws he does not mention the King-made law.

All this shows that the King's legislative powers were restricted within the narrowest bounds, and legal theory did not acknowledge his authority to impose any duties within the sphere of sacred law. But even for the little power that he exercised in restricting the liberties of his subjects, Manu had to bring forward an elaborate argument. That would tend to show that in making this provision Manu was making an innovation in legal theory, and that before him the constraining power of the King's commands, though it must have existed in practice, was unknown to legal theory. Old traditions were handed down, for ages, of Kings like Vena who had affected to override sacred law and impose rules of his own by Divine right (*h*). The discomfiture they suffered was an example to all Kings to keep the holy law sacred. That represents the feeling with which the people looked upon the idea of the King interfering with the laws of the people.

The recognition of the King's legislative powers by Manu shows that in his time all danger of a repetition of the Vena incident was gone. It was because Kings habitually obeyed the sacred law, and because the constitution of the state ensured that he would not interfere with it, that Manu and Yajnavalkya found it expedient to recognise his legislative powers. For in Manu

---

(*g*) II, 180. (*h*) Manu VII, 41.

and Yajnavalkya's time the King was reduced to more or less of an ornamental figurehead of the State, entirely in the hands of Brahmin ministers and advisers, and carrying on administration through them alone. Any authority conceded to the King could in practice only pass to the ministers.

It is significant that this slight recognition of the King's legislative powers has not been enlarged in subsequent times, and in all the elaborate disquisitions on the sources of law that we find amongst commentators, we do not see the King even once mentioned. Commentators like Raghavananda, moreover, attempt to explain away the text altogether. All this shows that idea of the King's legislative powers did not take root in ancient Indian polity. The development of law proceeded on quite other lines. How far this may have been due to the country being overrun by foreigners or to any other causes I shall not attempt here to guess.

§7 Accessory Sources of Law.

Besides the chief sources of sacred law, Hindu law books recognise certain accessories as likewise authoritative. These are the Puranas, Mimânsâ, Logic, the Vedangas, as well as self-satisfaction and reason.

Self-Satisfaction.

Self-satisfaction is mentioned as a valid source of rules of action only in matters where there is no law distinctly laid down, or where the law by reason of conflicting precepts or otherwise lays down an optional or alternative rule (*i*). It is thus not a source of law in the proper sense of the word, and its recognition as such is meant merely as a recognition of the liberty of the individual within the limits prescribed by law. We are too apt with modern notions to look upon such liberty as the primary fact and to regard law as mere limitation of such liberty. With archaic societies it was quite otherwise. With them the primary assumption was that every detail of life was settled by law either directly or through the authority of the various societies which exercised an all-pervading control over individuals. Liberty of the individual was an exception rather than the rule.

When Manu and Yajnavalkya laid down in express terms that self-satisfaction might lead to *dharma* in its own sphere just

(*i*) Yajnavalkya I. 7, and Mitakshara thereunder. Manu II, 3, and Medhatithi and Kulluka thereunder. Kulluka cites Garga as saying,

वैकल्पिके चात्मतुष्टिः प्रमाणम् ।

as well as the Vedas and Śmritis in their proper spheres, they were evidently representing a more advanced state of thought, when the choice of the actor himself held no inconsiderable place in the scheme of the religious life of the people. Manu and Yajnavalkya themselves lay down no limitations on the scope of *Atamatushti ;* but such limitations must be supplied from the scheme of life as conceived by them and Vijnaneswara is undoubtedly right when he restricts its sphere to cases which are not covered by an imperative text of law or Achara. Kulluka, and Medhatithi, however, go further and propose to read *Atmanah tushti* with *Sâdhunam* in Manu's text and to draw the conclusion that self-satisfaction is only to be conceded as a norm for the regulation of life to eminently virtuous men. This is an obviously strained interpretation, but at the same time it can not be conceived, as Kumarilaswami points out, that Manu could have contemplated the satisfaction of evil passions by *Atmatushti*. Manu and Yajnavalkya must have meant what was agreeable to the Soul, which was, in Hindu conception, identified solely with the highest and best in man and to which evil was entirely foreign.

Reason.

Reason too is rather a principle for the interpretation of law than one for initiating one (*j*). By putting it forward as a source of law, the authors were not recognising any principle like the Equity of Rome or England, but simply laying down that law was to be rationally interpreted and applied, and that where the law gave you no clear rule or there was a conflict, you had to apply your own judgment to decide what ought to be done. Yajnavalkya, in recognising the desire born of deliberation (*k*), was also obviously implying the same thing as Reason ; only, Narada, dealing, as he was with positive law or the law that the King was to administer contemplated a principle for determining objective rules, while Yajnavalkya was contemplating a subjective principle for the guidance of one's own conduct.

Reason has been plentifully applied in the commentaries for the elaboration of the law. Several principles of reason called

---

(*j*) The sphere of Reason is thus laid down by Narada :

धर्मशास्त्रविरोधेतु युक्तियुक्तोविधि:स्मृत: । Narada I, 40.

(*k*) सम्यक् सङ्कल्पज: काम: In Yajnavalkya I, 7. The Mitakshara interprets it thus सम्यक् सङ्कल्पाज्जात: शास्त्राविरुद्ध: काम:, यथा मया भोजन व्यतिरेकेणोदकं न पातव्यमिति ।

laukika nyayas nave been frequently applied by commentators and *Nibandha* writers. A reference may in this connection be made to the *dandâpupanyaya*, or argument *a fortiori* which has been frequently applied by the *Dayabhâga* in support of principles it enunciates. The artificial excesses to which Jimutavâhana carries this principle of argument is illustrated by his deduction of the limitations on the daughter's rights of enjoyment in property inherited from males from the fact that the *sastras* lay down the limitation on the higher right of the widow (*l*). Perhaps the most famous illustration of a *laukika nyaya* is the argument which has been called the *factum valet* doctrine (*m*). The error of the notion which identifies Jimutâvahana's argument with the *maxim factum valet quod fieri non debuit* has been thoroughly exposed (*n*). The argument here put forward was not a novel one but one which was familiar to every Indian jurist. It is that the substance of a thing must have precedence over accidents. Thus in discussing the relative authority of Sruti and Smriti, Kumarilaswami makes a distinction between texts which refer to the substance of an act and those that refer to its accidents (*o*). It is almost taken for granted that those relating to the essence of an act, no matter where found, must have precedence over those relating to the accidents. So too Mitra Misra makes use of the argument in the words of Jimutavahana himself in order to support the Mitakshara doctrine of absolute authority of women over property inherited by them against Jimutavahana's position to the contrary (*p*). What Jimutavahana meant by the argument was, not that a fact can not be altered, but that the essence of anything could be altered by texts relating to its accidents. The right of the property in the father was the thing (Vastu) and that was established by the *sastras* ; any texts relating to the disposition of that property would be matters affecting accidents of that Vastu. They would therefore be of no avail to curtail the nature of the thing ; so that, a rule which reasonably follows from the substance (property) itself, must have precedence over a rule relating to accidents no matter how authoritative.

These and numberless other illustrations of the application of reason in the evolution of rules of law show its proper

(*l*) Dayabhaga. Ch. XI, §ii, 30 (Colebrooke)

(*m*) Dayabhaga Ch. II, 30 (Colebrooke).

(*n*) In, for instance, Jogendra Nath Bhattacharjya's Hindu Law 2nd Ed.

(*o*) Tantravârtika (Benares Ed.) p. 118.

(*p*) Viramitrodaya Ch. III, i, 3, (G. C. Sâstri),

sphere. It could not be availed of to override a text of law but could be relied upon essentially for interpretation of the texts. The liberties taken with texts under the cover of interpretation are well-known. A notable principle of interpretation often availed of for purposes of explaining away the force of texts or of making recommendations obligatory was the *Samyoga-prithaktwa nyâya* (*q*). By means of devices like these the commentators and Nibandha writes expanded and developed, and, in other places, curtailed and abrogated, the laws of the Smritis in later days. Arguments like these might be assailed on the ground that the new rule evolved did not exist in the sacred law, and therefore it was not law. The text of Narada might however be relied upon to show that reasoning was also a valid source of law.

While Narada's text is the first explicit recognition of reason as a source of law it is clear that reason must have been always applied for the determination of law from the oldest times. In the oldest Dharmasastras extant we find elaborate arguments advanced in controverting the opinions of opponents and supporting those of the authors themselves. The arguments are not merely in the nature of literal or grammatical interpretation of texts but are attempts at what Ihering calls their 'logical' interpretation founded on reasoning. Perhaps the finest specimens of argumentation of this sort are to be found in Apastamba's Sutras. These show the long pedigree of the rational mode of interpretation and the tacit recognition of reason as a principle for the deduction of law from the oldest times.

Mimânsâ.

Another form of interpretation of sacred law is implied by the term Mimansa. By Mimansa or *Purva Mimansa* is meant the exegetic philosophy associated with the name of Jaimini and embodied in his sutras. The word Mimansa in its literal meaning implies settlement of disputes. We find not only this word but also a name for professors of Mimansa in Apastamba, Baudhâyana and Vasistha among Dharmasutras (*r*). But all the authors rely on rules of exegesis which have been elaborated in the Mimansa Darsana. They generally refer to these rules as *nyâyas* or arguments, a term which is still applied to them though when you speak of *Nyaya* system or the *naiyayika* as a proper

(*q*) See Jogendra Nath Bhattacharyya's Hindu Law 3rd Ed. p. 120.

(*r*) Apastamba II, 8, 3 ; Baudhâyana I, 1, 8. Vasistha III, 20.

name the logic of the *Akshapâda* school and, less usually, the Vaiseshika logic is meant.

The antiquity of the Mimansa rules is thus clear. When the texts of the Vedas and Brâhmanas were established as authorities, authoritative rules for their interpretation would naturally grow up, not necessarily as a system of hard and fast rules of a more or less artificial character, but as honest attempts to understand the meaning of the texts and to deduce rules from them by the application of reason.

In course of time however these rules would tend to grow fixed and when we find them referred to in the Dharmasutras, such an ossification of the rules has already taken place. Apastamba refers to these rules not as principles which might be open to question but as absolute verities. From Apastamba we also get it that there had already been before him men who were called Mimansakas who devoted their lives to the interpretation and systematisation of Vedic learning and, like the Sophists of Greece, had a number of maxims and principles which an irreverent man might regard as calculated "to make the worse appear the better reasoning." That they were held in great reverence by people and appealed to on questions of difficulty relating to Vedic precepts and rituals is apparent from Apastamba's regard for them.

It would seem however that even in Apastamba's time the exegetic philosophy of the Mimansists had not yet been built up into a system. This was done by Jaimini. The work of Jaimini clearly shows that there was not merely one school of interpreters of the Veda. It is true that the arguments of *Purvapakshas* that he sets up, which are elaborated with such apparent cogency by Sabaraswami and Kumarilaswami, were not necessarily arguments which had been actually put forward by any man, but might well have been conjured up by himself for the purpose of demolishing them and thereby establishing his own conclusions; but at the same time it is inconceivable that he was all along fighting imaginary opponents. Some of the *Purvapakshas* are so plausible, if not quite sound, that it is difficult to conceive that at Jaimini's time there was not a body of opinion holding that view. A reasonable view would seem to be to hold that there were differences between Mimansists with reference to the interpretation of the Vedas and Jaimini's work was merely an attempt to systematise their teachings according to the view of the author himself. In course of time Jaimini triumphed over his opponents and his system was established as the only school of Mimansa exegesis, just as the Vedânta of Bâdarâyana established itself as the only authoritative system embodying the philosophical teaching of the Upanishads which, as Deussen shows, represented at least two different shades of opinion (*s*).

The nature of the authority conceded to Mimansa as a source of law must have varied at different times. It had no sacred or occult authority behind it like the Sruti or Smriti. The only authority which it could therefore claim, to start with, was that founded on the reasonable character of the rules. Starting with the fundamental assumption that the Sruti was a consistent whole embodying all possible knowledge, the Mimansists sought to interpret the texts so as to satisfy reason and the authority of other texts. It was in doing so that they evolved from time to time different rules for the interpretation of Vedic texts as well as for supplementing them with rules otherwise obtained. They obtained currency on account of what was conceived to be their eminently reasonable character and as removing deadlocks caused by the conflict of laws. As they gained in public favour Mimansa rules tended to grow in fixity and certainty—they represented the traditional modes of interpretation of the Sruti. If we remember the vast power of constraint exercised by mere tradition in archaic society we shall be in a position to appreciate how the Mimansa thus grew into practical authority.

With all that however the authority of Mimansa in the Dharmasutras is only founded in theory upon its real and supposed reasonable character while its practical authority was founded on tradition and the habit of people to take traditional rules as also necessarily rational. It is only when we come to Yajnavalkya that we find Mimansa mentioned as authoritative. It was not permissible by his time to attempt to interpret the Vedas otherwise than by the principles of Mimansa exegesis. That is a position which Mimansa has ever since retained.

The original scope of the Mimansa did not contemplate law proper. It was concerned almost exclusively with rituals and other âchâras which are also founded on the same authorities as law proper. Then again, what was conceived to be its almost exclusive task was an exposition of Vedic texts alone. It also dwelt no doubt from very early times with Smriti and custom but only to consider the nature of the presumption of Vedic origin that arose from them. Even in Jaimini's time it did not purport to deal with Smritis except to discuss generally the scope of their

(*s*) Deussen: Religion and Philosophy of India. p. 239.

application and the nature of their authority. So far as interpretation of texts was concerned its sphere was confined to Sruti texts alone, as will be clear if we consider that even comparatively late commentators like Sabaraswami and Kumarilaswami illustrate the maxims of Mimansa almost exclusively by reference to Vedic texts.

The application of these principles to Smriti texts was the work of a later stage of thought when Smriti had been identified with the Dharmasastras and had been raised to a position of practical equality with the Veda as a source of law. At this stage, though, as we have seen, there were differences between commentators as to cases of conflict between Sruti and Smriti, they were unanimous that where there was no conflicting Sruti text Smriti had to be literally interpreted and applied. From this the conclusion was natural that like the Sruti they must be interpreted not from a mere commonsense point of view but on the lines of the authoritative rules of exegesis as expounded in the Mimansa. Already in Kumarilaswami we find that such an interpretation of Smriti texts is taken as a matter of cause. Commentators and authors of *Nibandha* works like Madhavâcharyya and Vijnaneswara and, judging from references to their works, other authors like Visvarûpa, Dhâreswara and others down to Raghunandana and Kulluka all unhesitatingly apply the authoritative exegesis of the Mimansa to Smriti texts. It was by this extension of the application of Mimansa to Smriti texts that the domain of law was affected by Mimansa. The important influence that the doctrines of Mimansa have however exercised on law in various ways would be apparent from even a most cursory view of these commentaries and Nibandhas.

Nyâya.

Nyaya and the Angas are mentioned by Yajnavalkya only to complete the list of recognised studies which are supposed to have any bearing on Vedic learning. We can find lists of such Vidyâs in most Smritis, though it is Yajnavalkya who mentions them as also sources of dharma. Thus for instance in the Upanishads, the Vedas as well as Purânas and Itihâsas are mentioned as studies pursued in those times (*t*). In Gautama we find Vedas, Angas, sayings of learned men, Itihâsa and Purâna (*u*). Kautilya

(*t*) ऋग्वेदं भगवोऽध्येमि यजुर्व्वेदं सामवेदमथर्व्ववेदं चतुर्थमितिहासं पञ्चमं पुराणं Upanishad cited in Tantravârttika, p. 126.

(*u*) वेदवेदाङ्गविद्वाक्येतिहासपुराणकुशलः । Gautama VIII 4—6.

in his Arthasâstra mentions several opinions on the subject (*v*). All these were studies which were regarded as the completion of Vedic knowledge and so far as any of them gave any guidance to conduct it was entitled to be looked upon as a foundation for dharma. Nyâya which, under the name of Anvikshaki, is mentioned from very old times, is one of such studies which was entitled to be called orthodox (*w*). The Nyâya (understanding by it the Akshapada Darsana) was not only the system of logic in ancient India. Leaving aside Mimansa and Vaiseshika which too were essentially sciences of reasoning, there was an elaborate and subtle logic of the Bauddhas, specially of the Mâdhyamikas and possibly also of Chârvâkas or Lokâyatikas (*x*). It may be that by mentioning Nyaya Yajnavalkya sought to exclude the application of principles of Bauddha and Lokayatika logic to matters of religion and law. The Mimansa had already been mentioned and the Vaiseshika was perhaps not developed as a separate school. The Nyâya school therefore represented at that time the only orthodox school of logic on matters not pertaining to the supra-sensible, for which latter the Mimansa furnished authority It would seem, in any case, that by Nyâya Yajnavalkya understood the Akshapada school, for in the general abstract sense of 'argument', it could not be counted a Vidya or Science. Of the practical application of principles of Nyâya philosophy as such we do not find any clear indications in the commentaries. Logic is used no doubt, but it would be difficult to say that the *laukika nyâyas* which were largely availed of were particularly identified with the Gautamiya school of logic.

Purânas and Itihâsas.

It is far different however with Purânas and Itihâsas which are mentioned from the very earliest times with reverence and appealed to for precedents and precepts in law. I have already referred to the text in the Upanishads which mention Purânas and Itihâsas as studies which go to the equipment of a thorough scholar. Gautama who is counted the earliest of extant lawgivers refers to them in the same strain. Apastamba actually

(*v*) p. 6.

(*w*) Kautilya understands by Anvikshaki, Sânkhya, Yoga and Lokâyata p. 6. In his time the word would thus seem to imply not logic, but philosophy ; and, possibly, his enumeration indicates that the Nyaya, Vaishe shika and Vedanta systems of philosophy had not yet been developed.

(*x*) These may be studied in Mâdhavâcharyya's *Sarvadarasana-sangraha*.

refers to them in many places for authority for his conclusions. That shows that even in his days Purânas were referred to as auxiliary sources of law.

It is difficult to say however what these Purânas actually were like and whether they can be properly identified with the extant Purânas. That all the extant Purânas are not ancient does not admit of a doubt, for, as Wilson points out, the enumeration of the eighteen Purânas, which is the traditional number given for them, differs in different Purânas (*y*). As a matter of fact more than eighteen Purânas are mentioned in all the works taken together. At the same time the usual theory that the Purânas in their present form are compilations not older than the 10th or 11th century A.D. cannot, as Bühler points out, be maintained (*z*). That there existed several Purânas so far back as the time of the Milinda Prasna is certain (*a*) and though allowance may have to be made for remodelling and recasting, such as, Bühler says, took place, yet it cannot be that the Purânas in their present developed form were very materially different from their originals. Though the time of the Purânas may not be ascertained, yet the result of recent researches on the subject seems to be that we cannot definitely say that the Purânas mentioned in the Dharmasutras were not the same works as go by that name to-day.

In any case there can be little doubt that Yajnavalkya was referring to the Purânas in their present form. Kumarilaswami frequently refers to the extant Purânas and all the later jurists draw their materials from these same works which they count as almost on a par with Smritis in the matter of law. Several important points of law have been settled by reference to the Purânas. Reference may be made to the prohibition of certain acts in the Kalijuga (*b*) and the limitation of the age of the son to be adopted which Nanda Pandita insists on, upon the authority of the Kalika Purâna (*c*). In these cases precepts are quoted

---

(*y*) Wilson : Introduction to the *Vishnu Purana*.

(*z*) Bühler : *Apastamba and Gautama* ; Introd : p. xxx note.

(*a*) V. Smith : *Early History of India*, p. 19 (1st Ed.) This portion of *Milinda Panha* is dated not later than 300 A.D. acc. to Smith.

(*b*) Text of Aditya Purana which after mentioning some rules of sacred law says

एतानि लोकगुप्त्यर्थं कलेरादौ महात्मभिः ।
निवर्तितानि कर्म्माणि व्यवस्थापूर्व्वकम् बुधैः ॥
समयश्चापि साधूनां प्रमाणम् वेदवद्भवेत् ॥

(*c*) See Dattaka Mimansa IV, 23.

from the Purânas, but by far the most important use that is made of Purânas and Itihâsas like the Mahabharata and the Ramayana is to derive authoritative precedents from them. An illustration may be found in the attempt of Nanda Pandita to establish the validity of adopted daughters on the authority of precedents from the Ramayana and the Mahabharata.

§8 Secular Customs.

So far we have dealt with dharma or sacred law which is principally established by Sruti, Smriti and sacred usages of the different kinds together with the auxiliary studies assisted by reason and self-satisfaction. But these did not exhaust all the law in ancient India. From the earliest times we find a recognition, side by side with the sacred law, of a body of secular laws founded partly on custom and partly on the authority of the various societies to which men belonged and partly developed in the secular sciences included under the name of Arthasastra.

"Dharma" is a word which has been used in different senses. In its application to duties and rules of conduct it has been used sometimes to imply all such rules and duties, and, at other times, in a more restricted sense. In the more restricted sense it means acts which lead to some occult benefit to the soul (*c*). The precepts of the Smritis were not merely laws in the sense of rules which subjects must be compelled by the King to follow, but also rules of conduct which would lead to elevation of the soul in the life hereafter. If we recall here what has been said before of the philosophy of life of the Hindus we shall find what exactly they understood by Dharma as law. The universe is conceived as a system of causes and effects in which nothing happens by accident. Every phenomenon is under the inexorable law of causality so that every act that is done leads to some consequences, not merely in this life, but also in some cases, in the long Hereafter to which one's existence is extended. Some acts such as eating, walking, sleeping, etc., done here will produce no consequences in the life hereafter, while others will have infallible consequences in the supersensible world. This consequence is the *Adrishta*, or *Apûrva* which, though called by

(*c*) Thus Haradatta explains Dharma as कर्मजन्योऽभ्युदयनिश्श्रेयसहेतुर-पूर्वाख्य आत्मगुणः धर्मः, understanding it as a property of the soul (Ujjala I, 1, 1).

different names, pervades the entire religious philosophy of the Hindus (*d*).

Of the apûrva consequences which acts may produce some may tend to elevate the soul in the life hereafter and take it towards the ultimate attainment of Bliss, others may produce the opposite consequences. The former would be *dharma* and the latter *adharma* or sin. Rules of conduct which dictate the performance of dharma are also called dharma. There may be acts however, as pointed out above, which have no apûrva consequences. These are not within the scope of dharma.

The dharmasâstras are concerned mainly with dharma ;—they do not, generally speaking, concern themselves with conduct which has no bearing on it. This dharma can only belong properly to the Aryas, that is, Brahmanas, Kshattriyas and Vaisyas. The Sudra can do acts productive of dharma only through the mediation of the Brahmana as a rule, though acts like giving alms which are also productive of merit are open to all classes. The Antyajas are incapable of dharma. The Vrâtyas and Vrishalas have fallen off from the path of dharma. It was not possible for them to produce those occult consequences that follow from the performance of acts enjoined by the Dharmasastras. With these therefore the sacred laws of Aryas have no concern.

There are, in the contemplation of the Smritis, countries and classes of people where and amongst whom sacred law does not exist (*e*). The names of these countries are differently given in different Smritis but there is a general agreement amongst them that the lands of Aryas lay in Northern India. In some of the lands devoid of Dharma the Arya is forbidden to dwell (*f*). To those countries the Smriti writers could not possibly conceive their sacred law as applying. In the land of the Aryas too there were classes of men who were incapable of dharma—the Antyajas (*g*) the abhisâstas, apapatras (*h*) and to a large extent

---

(*d*) Colebrooke : *Miscellaneous Essays* p. 343. Kishori Lal Sarkar : The *Mîmânsâ Rules of Interpretation* p. 35.

(*e*) See for instance Baudhayana I, 1, 2, 13—14.

(*f*) See for instance Baudhayana I, 1, 2, 14. आरट्टान् कारस्कराण् पुण्ड्रान् सौवीरान् कलिङ्गान् प्रानूनानिति च गत्वा पुनस्तोमेन यजेत सर्वपृष्ठया वा ।

(*g*) Including Chandâlas svapâks &c. and according to Manu also washermen and other people following lowly occupations.

(*h*) See Apastamba I, 21, 6 et seq , II 17, 20 ; Vasistha XX 16 ; Baudhayana I, 21, 15 ; II 2, 13 ; Manu X 51 refers to them along with Chandâlas and svapâks as those who must live outside the village.

the Sudras also. Then again even amongst Aryas there were certain matters which were of no moment spiritually. Thus for instance it is of no spiritual consequence at what hours a trader does his business or again what hours must be observed by journeymen labourers. On all these matters sacred law did not purport to provide.

Possibly we should never have heard how these matters were regulated in ancient law, by what laws the Vrishalas, Vrâtyas, Antyajas, Abhisâstas and Apapâtras were governed, were it not that it would be dharma for the king to maintain such laws as prevailed amongst them. Thus for instance, suppose the villagers make a rule by agreement that rents for land should be realised every six months. What the actual rule as to the time for the payment of rent is, is of no moment spiritually. But when that rule has been laid down it would be the duty of the king to respect and enforce that rule as a part of his dharma. So also it is immaterial for dharma what particular rules are made by a guild of traders for their own guidance. A true conception of the King's dharma of protection of his people requires, however, that he should enforce that rule against recalcitrant traders. Even in less innocent matters the same rule would apply. Thus, for instance, it was the duty of the king to do justice as amongst gamblers according to the rules of the game ascertained from gamblers themselves (*i*). Even a woman's wages of shame did not fall outside the scope of the king's dharma (*j*).

It is in connection with the king's dharma therefore that we are given a peep into the extensive domain of secular law that prevailed in ancient India. It is from the treatment of this subject that we know how a great many matters were regulated amongst Aryas themselves, how the affairs of Chandalas and other unclean people as well as of outcastes and Vrishalas and Vratyas were administered.

From the oldest times we find that the custom of the people furnishes the principal source of this secular law. Thus for instance, we find the king required to attend to desa, jati and kula dharma of persons even in respect of the clean castes (*k*).

(*i*) See Yajnavalkya II, 202 where gamblers are regarded as the only competent assessors and witnesses in these cases.

(*j*) See for instance Yajnavalkya II, 192 and another text cited by the Mitakshara thereunder.

(*k*) See notes below. Manu VIII, 3 requires the king to administer justice देशदृष्टैश्च शास्त्रदृष्टैश्च हेतुभिः Medhatithi understands देशदृष्ट to include customs which are विरुद्ध as well as those that are अविरुद्ध ।

Vasistha quotes Manu to show that these customs prevail in the absence of Sruti (*l*). This absence of Sruti may arise either because the matter does not appertain to sacred law at all, or because, though it does so, it has not been provided for by the Sruti. In the latter case the desadharma is a matter of sacred law ; in the former it is purely a matter of secular law.

Gautama in referring to the same sources makes them subject to the limitation that they should be unopposed to the Sruti (*m*) thus implying that, whether they appertain to the sacred law or not, they are referred to with regard to Aryas. He does not however impose any such limitation on the customs of herdsmen, husbandmen, traders, bankers and artisans on which they themselves are to pronounce (*n*). This was clearly because on matters affecting their various businesses the sacred law was not contemplated as applying. Possibly also this may have been due to the consideration that these men were not necessarily, if at all, Aryas amenable to sacred law (*o*).

It is clear from the Smritis themselves that the laws of the Smritis are meant for countries inhabited by Aryas. Even in these the Chandâla, the Abhisâsta and Apapâtra are outside the pale of sacred law. It was only the clean Aryas for whom the laws were meant. The Sudras, so sparingly mentioned, and then, only to emphasise their servile condition, were evidently not contemplated as participants in the sacred law except in so far as their status of inferiority was concerned.

For other countries not inhabited by Aryas the Smriti writers did not provide. These were inhabited by Vrishalas and Vrâtyas or Anâryas. They undoubtedly had their laws and customs. We are told that where a king conquers a new country he must maintain the laws and customs prevailing there (*p*). Now

---

(*l*) देशजातिकुलधर्म्मान् श्रुत्यभावेऽब्रवीन्मनुः Vasistha I, 17. Manu VIII, 205. Elsewhere Vasistha speaks of the duties of the king in the following terms : देशधर्म्म-जातिधर्म्म-कुलधर्म्मान् सर्व्वान वैताननुप्रविश्य राजा चतुरो वर्णान् स्वधर्म्मे स्थापयेत् ।

(*m*) देशजातिकुलधर्म्माः आम्नायैरविरुद्धाः ; Gauṭama XI, 20.

(*n*) कृषिवणिक-पाशुपाल्य-कुसीद-कारवः स्वे स्वे वर्गे ; Ibid XI, 21.

(*o*) It seems that the artisans were principally Sudras. Kautilyȧ refers to कारुकुशीलवकर्म्म and वार्त्ता as special occupations of Sudras. Kautilya, Arthasastra (Mysore) p. 7.

(*p*) स एव नृपतेर्धर्म्मः स्वराष्ट्र परिपालने ।
तमेव कृत्स्नमाप्नोति परराष्ट्रं वशं नयन् ॥

if the king conquered a non-Aryan territory or one supposed to be inhabited by Vrâtyas, it is clear that he would be expected to maintain the laws and customs prevailing amongst them no matter whether they were approved by the sacred law or not. *Ex hypothesi* these lands were inhabited by men who had renounced the sacred law and who had not the status requisite for the participation in sacred law without *prayaschitta*. Therefore the king would have to recognise these laws as binding though they might not lead to *Apûrva* consequences.

It is quite clear that the customs in these matters were not enforced on the same principle as sacred custom which governed the practices of Aryans in the matter of the sacred law. We have seen before the stringent limitations imposed upon that custom which can raise the presumption of a Srauta origin. The customs of husbandmen and artisans, not to speak of Chandâlas and outcvastes, Vrâtyas and Vrishalas, could not possibly be counted as Sishtâchara which raised such presumption. These customs were therefore recognised merely because they were customs; they were rather suffered to exist than positively ordained. So too although the agreement of a number of heretics could not possibly be placed on the footing of the resolutions of a Parishad, yet, as we shall presently see, they were recognised as having binding force within the community of heretics themselves.

In the older Dharmasastras we find mention of communities of excommunicated sinners with whom sacred law has no concern, Chandâlas foreign to sacred law and communities of herdsmen, husbandmen etc. mentioned incidentally as managing their own affairs. Beyond that we know very little about the nature of their laws. The scope of these Dharmasastras was primarily to furnish to each Arya a personal code of rules of Dharma and to the king amongst others. In the metrical Dharmasastras however the scope of Smritis has considerably expanded and Manu in his general summary of topics dealt with in his work, mentions side by side with the usual topics of sacred law the desa, jati and kula Dharmas as well as pâshanda and gana Dharmas (*e*). Pâshandas are explained by Medhatithi to be those who follow

---

यस्मिन्देशे य आचारः व्यवहारः कुलस्थितिः ।
तथैव प्रतिपाल्योऽसौ यदा वशमुपागतः ॥ Yajnavalkya I, 342—343
So Vishnu III, 42, परदेशावाप्तौ तद्देशधर्मान् नोच्छिन्द्यात् ।

(*q*) देशधर्माञ्जातिधर्मान् कुलधर्मांश्च शाश्वतान् ।
पाषण्डगणधर्मांश्च शास्त्रेऽस्मिन्नुक्तवान् मनुः ॥ Manu I, 118.

practices forbidden in the sacred law, and ganas, as assemblies of herdsmen, artisans etc.

These Manu deals with under the section dealing with what is called *Samvidvyatikrama* or *Samayabheda* (*r*). There he lays down the punishment ordained for one who, being a member of the society, breaks any compact arrived at by it and he mentions among the various societies to which this law applies the grâma, desa and sangha. Medhâtithi explains *grâma* as the assembly of members of a village, *desa* as an assembly of many villages and *sangha* as a community of men having any common property though coming from different races, and illustrates it by referring to communities of Bhikshus, of traders and learned men (*s*). Obviously Manu understood the same rule as applying to the communities of *pâshandas*.

Yâjnavalkya deals with the law of communities more fully, and after giving some recommendations as to how the affairs of any community ought to be looked after, and providing for punishments for offences against the community and rules settled by agreement amongst them, he lays down that this law applies to *srenis*, *naigamas*, *pakhandis* and *ganas* further ordains that their old laws should be maintained (*t*). The Mitâkshara explains srenis as assemblies of persons following the same trade or art, naigamas as assemblies of heretic sects like the pâshupatas who acknowledge a qualified authority of the Veda but would not admit its eternal existence, pâkhandi as assemblies of those who do not acknowledge the authority of the Vedas, such as Buddhists, gana as a general term for all associations including persons pursuing the same calling (*u*).

Narada is more comprehensive in the enumeration of the societies. He names *pâshandi* (or pâkhandi) *naigama*, *Sreni*, *Puga*

(*r*) Manu VIII 219—221.

यो ग्रामदेशसंघानां कृत्वा सत्येन संविदम् ।

विसम्वदेन्नरो लोभात्तं राष्ट्राद्विप्रवासयेत् ॥ Manu VIII 219.

(*s*) Medhatithi comments : ग्रामासमुदयोग्राम:,तन्निवासिनो मनुष्या गृह्यन्ते, तेषामेव सम्विद: सम्भवात् ; एवं ग्रामससुदयो देश, संघ एकधर्म्मानुगतानां नानादेशवासिनां नाना-जातीयानामपि प्राणिनांसमूह:, यथा भिक्षूणां संघो, वणिजां संघश्चातुर्व्विद्यानां संघ इति ।

(*t*) श्रेणीनैगमपाखण्डिगणानामप्ययं विधि: ।

भेदश्चैषां नृपो रक्षेत् पूर्व्ववृत्तिञ्च पालयेत् ॥ Yajnavalkya II, 192.

(*u*) एकपण्यशिल्पोपजीविन: श्रेणय: । नैगमा: ये वेदस्य आप्तप्रणीतत्वेन प्रामाण्य-मिच्छन्ति पाशुपतादय: । पाखण्डिणो ये वेदस्य प्रामाण्यमेव नेच्छन्ति, नग्ना: सौगतादय: । गणो व्रात: आयुधीयानामेककर्म्मोपजीविनामेषां चतुर्व्विधानामप्ययं विधि: ।

vrâta and *gana* as well as villages (*v*). With the exception of sreni and puga, which imply associations of men indifferently, all these associations are of men belonging to the lower classes and heretics. Narada's text therefore may be relied upon to show that the topics of law called *samvidvyatikrama* was pre-eminently meant for the administration of justice between persons not within the pale of sacred law.

In Manu, Narada and Yajnavalkya this became the principal object of this branch of law. But there is little doubt that this was an extension of the law as it applied to Aryas also from the earliest times. We have seen before that Gautama speaks of customs of societies which might be those of Aryas. Kautilya too provides for the punishment for the violation of resolutions of communities irrespective of whether they are of Aryas or not and concludes the section dealing with this matter by saying, "By this the violation of the resolutions of desa, jati, kula and sangha, has been explained" (*w*). It seems therefore that any rule settled by Arya societies in matters not relating to sacred law was from the earliest time recognised as law which the king was enjoined to enforce. The same rule was applied to communities other than those of Aryas. The importance assigned to heretics and unclean people in Manu, Narada and Yajnavalkya shows that between the time of the Dharmasutras and that of the metrical Smritis the heretic sects and non-Arya people had risen in importance sufficiently to demand some recognition at the hands of law-givers. It does not show however that their affairs were not managed from the earliest times by the customs prevailing among them and by the resolutions of their communities. On the other hand, as I have observed before, we should be more justified in holding that these communities with their powers of legislation and coercion must have existed before the organisation of the state with the king at its head. Of important Chandâla communities we hear from the earliest times. The stories of Trisanku

---

(*v*). पाषण्डि नैगमादीनां स्थितिः समय उच्यते ।
समयस्यानपाकर्म्म तद्विवादपदं स्मृतम् ॥
पाषण्डि-नैगम-श्रेणी-पूग-व्रात-गणादिषु ।
संरक्षेत् समयं राजा दुर्गे जनपदे तथा ॥
यो धर्म्मः कर्म्म यच्चैषामुपस्थान विधिश्च यः ।
यच्चैषां वृत्त्युपादानमनुमन्येत तत्तथा ॥ Narada Tit. X, 1—3.

(*w*) Kautilya : Arthasastra p. 173
तेन देशजातिकुलसंघानां समयस्यानपाकर्म्म व्याख्यातं ।

and Guhaka show that they were not a quite negligible element in Ancient Indian society.

We get it then that persons outside the pale of sacred law, as well as persons within it, in matters of no spiritual importance, were governed by their own customs and by the ordinances of their own communal organisations. Narada enjoins the King to maintain their samayas as well as whatever was their religious customs and institutions. These were to be maintained not from the same considerations as sacred custom of the Smritis but merely as customary.

I have spoken of these as secular customs. They were enforced as such, but it would be wrong to say that the rules thus enforced had necessarily no religions bearing. Heretics and unclean people had their own religions and the customs they followed might, to them, appear to be founded on religion. Only the Aryas would not recognise their religion as the true religion and if they enforced the rules it would be only as parts of secular law.

It could not be that the vast body of non-religious customary law that was thus recognised should for ever exist side by side with the holy law of the Aryas without their exercising some influence upon one another. On the one hand the sacred law itself may have been enriched by additions from the customary law and, on the other, the secular customs, specially among unclean communities, may have been very largely influenced by the sacred law. In this way mutual interaction would very likely make the two sets of laws approximate to one another. Thus for instance it may just be that the various inferior forms of marriage recognised in the Smritis may have got into vogue amongst Aryas by imitation of their less advanced neighbours. We get it as a fact that the religious form of marriage was a common institution amongst all Aryans. We find also that marriage by purchase was the only form of marriage recognised by the Assyrians (Ashurs) who were evidently not unknown in India. Among the various aboriginal tribes such as Khasias and Mundas we yet find marriage by capture, actual or pretended, as the only form of marriage. It is quite conceivable therefore that, while the Aryans when they came to India knew the religious forms of marriage alone, they appropriated the other forms of marriage from neighbouring races and the aboriginal tribes.

The influence of Aryan law on the customary law of inferior classes is clearer still. A student of the customs of unclean castes, as well as of provinces which have not been permeated by Smriti law, would be struck by the similarities between Smriti law and the customs, with reference to laws of inheritance, adoption, marriage, status of women and the like (x). On these matters the law was evidently largely moulded by the laws of the Aryas. It is always a point of honour with classes of people more or less low on the social scale to imitate customs of the superior classes of society. We find illustrations of such imitation everywhere. The plebians of Rome were keen on celebrating their marriages according to civil law rites, possibly, not so much because of any practical disadvantages in their own forms as because the patrician marriage was ever so much more dignified even in their eyes than their own. Even in our own times in India we find castes and communities with an inferior status anxious to imitate practices of a superior class for the sake of dignity. Thus we find communities, among whom widowhood is not half as rigorous a discipline as in the upper classes, introducing among their widows the same rigorous rules as govern the life of a higher class widow. Communities among whom widow-remarriage was practised within living memory are fast giving up the practice because it is not counted proper amongst the higher castes. Communities who have for ages lived without the sacred thread are now very keen about adopting it because that is a sign of dignity and high social status. These movements are all impelled by the same motives from which the persons outside the sacred law in India imitated the holy law of Aryas in the past.

Learned European scholars have been struck with the absence of all religious significance, among certain classes, of acts which are counted essentially religious in the Smritis. Upon this they have built up the theory that the sacred import of the act was a later addition to the secular laws of the people. Thus for instance adoption is, as Rattigan points out, a secular institution in the Punjab, and, we may say, among the lower classes everywhere. The reason for this however is not that the secular act of adoption was prior to the religious significance now attached to it. It would be more proper to explain the phenomenon as an imitation by these people of the religious act of adoption prevailing among the Aryas. They might by such imitation take a son to themselves but could not produce the spiritual relationship produced by the accompanying ceremonies which could only be performed by Aryas. Thus the act of adoption dropped its formal character as well as its spiritual significance when it was adopted by the people outside the sacred law just as institutions of the Jus Gentium in

(x) The customs of the Punjab in Rattigan's *Digest* would funish an interesting basis for comparison. Rattigan himself notices this fact.

Rome dropped the formal and, presumably, religious character which they had in old civil law. That this would be the proper explanation of the phenomenon would seem clear if we remember that the essential fact in a juristic act is first conceived under an elaborate form from which it is disentangled only in the course of time. A consideration of the nature of adoption shows, as we have seen, that it must have owed its first beginning to the essentially spiritual relation of father and son. The various ceremonies connected with the conception, birth and the subsequent samskâras of the son emphasised this essentially spiritual relationship with the son and created it in the case of one who was not the begotten son. It was through the religious ceremonies and their spiritual import alone that the adopted son would have got into the status of a son. We can understand the inclusion of the Kshettraja, Gudhotpanna or Kanina son in the family from entirely natural causes, but the position of the adopted son was so anomalous that we cannot conceive of its having been acknowledged without the extension of the spiritual relationship to him. It would be proper therefore to suppose that the institution of adoption first received recognition by the instrumentality of a fiction of a sacred law and that the shedding of its religious character in some communities was a later fact.

The history of the development of Hindu law is to very large extent a history of this mutual interaction of these two bodies of laws existing in India from very ancient times. In this history we should also have to count the influence exerted by large bodies of foreign customs which must have been imported along with the successive raids of the Greeks, Sakas, Huns and the various Mongolian tribes in ancient times. The impact of Indian civilisation with that of Assyrians, Persians and even Arabs must also be counted. It is only when we have taken account of all these that we may get an insight into the inner history of Hindu law.

The existence and recognition in India at all times of a body of laws not founded on Sruti, Smriti and sacred custom throw a not quite pleasant light on the history of the administration of Hindu law by British Indian courts. To Nelson must be given the credit of having first drawn pointed attention to the diversities of customs in Southern India which made it absurd to seek to apply to them the Hindu law, i.e, the general provisions of the Smriti law, as the common law of the country (y). Mr. Justice

(y) In his *View of Hindu Law*, *Prospectus on a Scientific Study of Hindu Law* and other writings.

Holloway remarked on a notable occasion on "the grotesque absurdity of applying the Hindu law to the Maravers" (*z*). The absurdity however did not lie in the application of the Hindu law or rather the Smriti law, but in the want of proper understanding of that law. When the Smritis lay down the law of marriage, inheritance or adoption they contemplate it as applying only to Arya countries. For others the law is laid down by the customs and resolutions of the communities themselves. That is the plain import of the Smriti, and, so far as commentaries go, there is nothing to show that they contemplated anything else. When therefore you apply the law relating to joint families or inheritance to persons like the Maravers you are going against and not properly applying the law of the Smritis or the commentaries.

This failure to recognise the proper scope of the provisions of Smritis with reference to the various topics of law has led to a great deal of confusion of ideas in many places. A notable instance is furnished by the dictum that, according to Hindu law, a clear proof of usage will outweigh the written law (*a*). This is at best a half-truth and even as such, an imperfect expression of it. The fact is that the scope of usage is different in sacred and secular law. While in the former it has only a restricted scope, in the latter it is absolutely supreme. Usage will not outweight a text of law where one exists and where one really applies, for it would apply only within the sphere of sacred law. But in the vast domain of law outside the sacred laws of the Aryas it has unrestricted scope.

The mischief has been largely caused by the fact that the only parts of Hindu law generally studied by those who had the moulding of Hindu law under British rule was the portion on inheritance together with something of the law of marriage. Even among the Pandits who advised the judges, the study of the Smritis as living law had ceased, except with reference to âchara, prâyaschitta, marriage, inheritance and such other topics. The Smriti law had long ceased to be the law of the land and it was not studied as such. British Indian law sought to apply it as such and from a confusion of the scope of the law as laid down in the Smritis, rules which were meant to apply within strictly limited spheres were taken far beyond their scope. If the section on *samvidvyatikrama* in Manu, Narada and Yajnavalkya had been studied properly this grievous error would not have occurred.

(*z*) 6 M. H. C. R. 310.

(*a*) *Per* Sir James Colvile in *Collector of Madura v. Muthu Ramalinga* 12M. I. A. at p. 436.

§9 Commentaries & Nibandhas.

I have dealt with the sources of law in ancient India. I have not mentioned the commentaries and nibandhas which in modern times carry the greatest practical authority and which have been recognised on the high authority of the Privy Council as being of more weight than the Smritis themselves (*b*). That is because they fall outside the scope of my subject which is concerned with ancient India alone. Besides, commentaries and nibandhas, however great their practical authority, are not legal sources of law. I shall however conclude this thesis with a short statement of the nature of their real authority.

There has been some amount of general misapprehension as to the nature of the authority of these works. That for practical purposes works like the Mitakshara, Dayabhaga, the Mayûkhas and Raghunandana's Tattwas excercise an enormous influence and almost arrogate to themselves the position of primary sources of law is undoubted. But this authority is not of such a character as not to bear challenge.

These works might in fact be compared with the works of Bracton and Glanvill which English lawyers have for ages looked upon with the utmost reverence but which, at the same time, they would not call legal sources of law. So Raghunandana's work has for a pretty long time been the exclusive source of the legal learning of the Bengal Pandit. At the same time, supposing that a Pandit from Dravida comes and challenges Raghunandana's position in one of the dialectical combats that we used to have in the past, the Bengal Pandit could not fall back on the authority of Raghunandana but would have to support his arguments by reference to Sruti and Smriti. So that, underlying the practical authority of these works, there is the fundamental presumption that they represent the correct view of the Smritis. That presumption was very strong, but it might be rebutted and it is nothing unusual to find a commentator or follower of a great nibandha departing from his authority. Thus for instance both Raghunandana and Sreekrishna have had occasion to depart from the opinions of the Dayabhaga which they comment on.

The practical authority of the various works was the result of the influence of the various seats of learning which are perhaps the remnants of the Vedic Parishads. In places like Benares, Mithila, Nadia and Vikrampur important seats of learning

(*b*) In the *Ramnad case* 12 M. I. A. at p. 436.

flourished. There all scholars flocked for instruction and when they had finished their education they spread over the entire province. Naturally they would carry with them the traditional teachings of the school which found favour in their Alma Mater and if there was any one book which was the favourite at these centres of learning they would endeavour to have with them a copy of that *Opus majus*. These men would give vyavathas on all matters that concerned villagers and thus gradually mould the practical law in accordance with the teachings of their particular authority. That would be how the authority of a work like that of Raghunandana would spread over an entire province. In other cases we find commentaries and laws published under the authority of kings or by their ministers who helped to administer justice. It is easy to see that such works would soon gain considerable authority within the dominions of the King (*c*).

It was thus that commentaries and nibandhas came into existence. They carried great weight corresponding to the eminence of their authors, but were not absolutely conclusive on any point.

(*c*) It is possible however that the importance of the compilation of works under the authority of King may have been exaggerated e.g. by Jolly in his T. L. Lectures. For, if we are right in the picture of Indian society I have given before, the constraint exercised by communal groups and seats of learning would, generally speaking, be at least as considerable as that referrible to the King. As a general rule, adjudication of disputes outside the capital would very rarely go up to the King or the King's courts and, since it would be by this means alone that the King's law could spread, the expansion of it would not be very great without the aid of centres of learning.